CULTURES OF THE WORLD

GREECE

Jill DuBois

MARSHALL CAVENDISH
New York • London • Sydney

Reference edition published 1993 by
Marshall Cavendish Corporation
2415 Jerusalem Avenue
P.O. Box 587
North Bellmore
New York 11710

© Times Editions Pte Ltd 1992

Originated and designed by
Times Books International, an imprint of
Times Editions Pte Ltd

Printed in Singapore

Library of Congress Cataloging-in-Publication Data:
DuBois, Jill, 1952–
    Greece / Jill DuBois.
        p. cm.—(Cultures Of The World)
    Includes bibliographical references and index.
    Summary: Introduces the geography, history, economics, culture, and people of the Mediterranean country of Greece.
    ISBN 1-85435-450-7
    1. Greece—Juvenile literature [1. Greece.]
I. Title. II. Series.
DF717.D83 1992
949.5—dc20   91–41004
                        CIP
                         AC

Cultures of the World

Editorial Director	Shirley Hew
Managing Editor	Shova Loh
Editors	Roseline Lum
	Goh Sui Noi
	June Khoo Ai Lin
	Siow Peng Han
	Leonard Lau
	Tan Kok Eng
	MaryLee Knowlton
Picture Editor	Yee May Kaung
Production	Edmund Lam
Design	Tuck Loong
	Ang Siew Lian
	Lee Woon Hong
	Lo Yen Yen
	Ong Su Ping
Illustrators	Suzana Fong
	Kelvin Sim
Cover Picture	Rick Strange (APA Photo Agency)

INTRODUCTION

Greece, the oldest civilization in Europe, is the inspiration for all of Western civilization. The ancient Greeks laid the foundations of philosophy and science, created art forms and developed an intellectual and academic life that remains an ideal today.

Yet, 2,500 years later, the people of Greece are striving to regain a role of world importance for their beloved country. Though it was the birthplace of democracy, Greece has endured political and cultural oppression for hundreds of years and tried nearly every form of government in its long and colorful history.

The Greeks' deep sense of cultural unity and respect for traditions have preserved this rich society through invasions, political strife and wars. And despite all these adversities, Greece remains one of the most linguistically and culturally homogeneous nations of the world.

As part of the *Cultures of the World* series, this book will familiarize you with the attitudes and lifestyles of the proud, opinionated and hospitable people of Greece and the beautiful but sometimes hostile terrain on which they live.

ATHENS

CONTENTS

The gleaming white houses are typical of Greek island architecture.

3 INTRODUCTION

7 GEOGRAPHY
Topography • Climate • Flora • Fauna • Greek cities

17 HISTORY
The city-states and classical period • The golden age of Athens • The Macedonian conquest • The Roman republic • Frankish and Venetian occupation • Ottoman rule • The Greek kingdom • Post World War II developments • Democracy restored

31 GOVERNMENT
Independence to World War II • Military dictatorship • Democracy returns • Armed Forces

37 ECONOMY
Tourism • Agriculture • Fishing • Sailing the seven seas • Industry • Mining

47 GREEKS
Population trends • Minority groups • Social divisions

57 LIFESTYLE
All in the family • The godfather • Patrida • Patronage • Philoxenia • Of men and women • Philotimo • Education • Among friends • Love is in the air • Tying the knot • Baby boom • Death rituals

71 RELIGION
Church authorities • Religion in modern Greece • Wearing the robes • The monastic life • Sunday at church • Superstitions

CONTENTS

81 LANGUAGE
The alphabet • Dialects

87 ARTS
Literature in ancient Greece • Art and architecture in ancient Greece • Modern arts

101 LEISURE
Folk music • Folk dancing • Sports • Movies and television • Theater

109 FESTIVALS
Festivals of local patron saints • Christmas • St. Basil's day • Epiphany • Name day • Independence and Ochi day • Easter season

117 FOOD
Traditional food and drink • The open-air market of Athens • Cooking in villages • Mealtimes • Table manners and social graces • Yiassas

124 MAP OF GREECE

126 QUICK NOTES

127 GLOSSARY AND BIBLIOGRAPHY

128 INDEX

The winding road reflects the mountainous geography of Greece.

GEOGRAPHY

GREECE IS THE SOUTHERNMOST COUNTRY IN EUROPE. Also known as the Hellenic Republic, the country occupies the lower part of the Balkan peninsula. It is bordered by the Aegean Sea to the east, the Mediterranean to the south and the Ionian Sea to the west. Toward the north, Greece shares its boundary with Albania, Yugoslavia and Bulgaria. Its nearest neighbor to the east is Turkey.

Greece is approximately the size of New York state. It has a surface area of 50,944 square miles, which includes the mainland and approximately 2,000 Greek islands. About 170 of these islands are inhabited while some others are merely outcrops of rock. Nearly 80% of Greece is mountainous and only 30% of the land is arable.

Greece is often divided into nine geographic regions. There are six mainland regions and three insular, or island, regions. The mainland regions are Thrace, Macedonia, Epirus, Thessaly, Central Greece and the Peloponnesus. Insular regions include the Ionian Islands, Crete and the Aegean Islands.

Opposite: **Along coastal lowlands and between mountain valleys violet pansies bloom in the warm Mediterranean climate of Greece.**

Left: **Twilight over the Ionian island of Corfu.**

7

TOPOGRAPHY

The country's predominant geographic feature is mountains which cover three-quarters of the mainland. The mountain ranges originate in Albania, Bulgaria and Yugoslavia and stretch all the way to the southern coast of Greece. The Olympus Range along the northeast coast and the Pindus Mountains running north to south are the most well-known. Mount Olympus, which is famous in ancient Greek literature and mythology, is the highest mountain at 9,570 feet.

There are very few rivers and lakes in Greece. None of them are navigable, so these rivers cannot be used for transporting people or goods. Many of the small rivers even dry up in the summer! The most important rivers in Greece are the Axiós, Evros and Strymón. The country's largest lakes are all located in the northern region. They are Ioánnina, Kastoría and Prespa.

GREECE IS GROWING

It seems that Greece is stretching. Navigational satellites measuring the movements of monuments in a geological surveying network have shown that southern Greece has stretched more than three feet from north to south in the 100 years since the original survey was made. According to British and Greek scientists, the Peloponnesus has moved in a southwesterly direction from the mainland.

In 1890 the positions of the monuments were ascertained by triangulation, a scientific method of measuring the network of triangles into which the earth's surface is divided for surveying. But, because satellites were not used, the overall orientation and position of the network was not determined. However, measurements of magnetism in ancient rocks indicate that some clockwise rotation has occurred over the last several million years.

About 60% of the expansion is attributable to regional earthquake activity during the last century. Much seismic action has occurred in the Gulf of Kórinthos, which is the area between the Greek mainland and the Peloponnesus.

CLIMATE

The climate of Greece is typical of other Mediterranean countries such as Italy and Spain. The lowland summers are hot and dry; the winters are generally cold and damp. But, because of great variations in the heights of land above sea-level and its closeness to the sea, there are often local differences in climate. For example, the average winter temperature in the capital city of Athens is 47 F, but in other parts of the country it is extremely cold. On the southern coast of Crete it is warm enough to swim almost every day of the year. In the summer the normal high temperature is 99 F, but in Thrace, Macedonia and Thessaly the summer temperatures are cool.

Rainfall too varies greatly from region to region. Thessaly can have as little as 1.5 inches of rainfall per year while parts of the western coast can receive as much as 50 inches per year. Frost and snow are rare in the lowlands, but the mountains are covered with snow in the winter.

Fiery-red geraniums thrive in the sunny weather of Greece.

FLORA

Many interesting flowers and shrubs can be found throughout Greece. Some of the common blossoms that are characteristic of the country include tulips, laurel, acacia, bougainvillea, hibiscus, jasmine, mimosa, oleander and sycamore. Wild flowers such as anemone and cyclamen are found in areas that are higher than 4,000 feet, while mosses and lichen grow in regions above 5,000 feet.

In the north and at higher altitudes, forests of Grecian fir and black pine thrive, giving way to deciduous trees such as oak and chestnut at lower altitudes. Pines, planes and poplars thrive along Greece's rocky slopes and coastal plains.

Many grains have been grown in Greece as far back as prehistoric times. Wheat, oat, barley, millet and spelt are native to Greece. Grains such as these are made into staple food such as bread. But because of the shortage of arable land, Greece does not produce enough grains to feed its population and must import them from other countries.

Grapes are an important crop, some of which are grown for their juice which is made into wine. Currants are another grape product. In fact, the word "currant" is derived from the phrase "Corinth grape." Grapevines also provide pleasant shaded areas in gardens and courtyards. Other fruits grown in Greece include apricots, dates, figs, citrus fruits and peaches. A native fruit that is also a valuable export is the olive.

The goat is an important source of food. Its meat is used in many Greek dishes and goat's milk is used for making cheese as well as a daily beverage.

FAUNA

Wildlife includes boar, European black bear, lynx, jackal, chamois (a goat-like antelope), deer, fox, badger and weasel. Birds of the region are hawk, egret, nightingale, partridge, pheasant, stork and turtledove.

Some of what is perhaps Greece's most interesting wildlife is found in the sea. The murex, for example, is a shellfish that releases a purple dye that was used thousands of years ago to color the clothing of the very rich. Octopuses live along the shore, hiding behind rocks to protect their soft bodies. They range in size from very tiny to more than 14 feet across. Even larger are the squid which can grow as long as 75 feet! Another aquatic creature that is common in the warm Mediterranean waters surrounding Greece is the dolphin. For many years Greek artists have captured the likeness of this gentle mammal in paintings and carvings.

GREEK CITIES

ATHENS   For many years Athens was the center of ancient Greek civilization. But during the time of the Turkish occupation of Greece, Constantinople (today's Istanbul) became the capital city attracting trade and artists as it grew in importance. Athens was left behind.

As a result, by the time Greece regained its independence in the 19th century, Athens had been reduced to a sprawling village. However, since becoming the capital of free Greece, Athens has grown in population from 10,000 to more than 4 million. The city has grown so much that its boundaries have been stretched all the way to the port of Piráeus, which is now considered to be a part of greater Athens.

The rapid growth of the capital has resulted in some typical urban problems. There is little open space in Athens because buildings that were hastily erected in the last 30 years are quite close to one another. There are also few trees to adorn the streets. Pollution has become a rather serious problem. The smog is so deadly that during a 10-day heat wave in the summer of 1987, 1,000 deaths were attributed to the poor quality of air.

Modern Athens lies in a valley between four notable hills: the Acropolis, Mount Pentelicus, Mount Hyméttus and Mount Lycabéttus.

Omónoia Square is the commercial hub of the city. Eight streets branch out from the fountained square, each teeming with traffic. Pedestrians can escape from the hustle and bustle to an underground arcade which houses a subway. This busy subway transports workers and visitors to the various suburbs surrounding the capital city.

The village square of Athens is Syntagma (Constitution) Square, which faces the Parliament Building. It is a popular place for Athenians to meet over coffee at the many outdoor cafés. Outside the central downtown area, older streets with narrow sidewalks are filled with merchandise offered by shopkeepers and street vendors alike. The combination of sellers, pedestrians, cars and buses makes for a very congested and spirited environment.

A spin-off from the tourist industry, this flea market in Athens sells all forms of souvenirs and handicrafts for the home.

The old quarter of Athens is known as the Pláka. There, houses with red-tiled roofs occupy a slope on the Acropolis. Many restaurants or *tavérnas* are located in this area, and tourists and local residents enjoy good food and lively entertainment until the early hours of the morning.

The modern center of Thessaloníki is framed by older Byzantine and Turkish buildings. The White Tower, one of Thessaloníki's landmark monuments, is a reminder of the city's important role through the centuries.

THESSALONÍKI The second largest city of Greece, which is often called the northern capital, is Thessaloníki. This city was founded by Alexander the Great's brother-in-law, Cassander, who named the settlement for his Thessaly-born wife. It is strategically located on the Aegean Sea and this enviable position has made the town a prime target for invaders. During the long reign of the Turks, Thessaloníki outranked Athens in terms of cultural development and commercial significance. Today, it is the second most important port in Greece.

Throughout the city are monuments left by its many invaders. For example, the Venetian White Tower, part of a seawall built in the 15th century, remains near the waterfront. The Triumphal Arch erected by the Romans to honor Emperor Galerius in the 4th century stands proudly among modern commercial buildings and urban housing. Via Egnatia, built by the Romans to link Constantinople with Rome, is still the main thoroughfare of Thessaloníki, though it has been widened and modernized over the centuries. Some of the most cherished examples of Greek Christian art survive in the city's stately Byzantine churches.

The city itself is often referred to as a museum of Byzantine art. The oldest church is the Church of St. George, which has a splendid mosaic-covered dome. The church has been converted to a museum where classical and Byzantine music recitals are occasionally held. Another noteworthy church is the Basilica of Agia Sofia (Holy Wisdom) which is similar to a church of the same name in Istanbul.

The waterfront in Thessaloníki is a favorite spot for residents to take an evening stroll. Alongside the merchant shipping vessels are fishing boats, which local children call ducks.

As dusk falls on Greece, the harsh light gives way to a cool hue. Evenings are times of leisure when people go for long walks or simply enjoy the cool sea breeze.

PIRÁEUS Though considered a part of greater Athens, Piráeus is officially a separate city. One of the major ports of the Mediterranean, it is also a vital industrial city with hundreds of factories.

Like Athens, Piráeus was just a small village when Greece won its independence. It is now home to the country's merchant navy, the third largest in the world. And although it is a major port of call, there is still the easy-going lifestyle of a big fishing village.

Open-air cafés dot the waterfront between the Naval Museum and the remains of the Archeological Museum. There is a modern amphitheater that presents ancient dramas and folk dance recitals, with majestic mountains providing a spectacular backdrop for the audience.

Piráeus, however, is more than a seaport. More than half of Greece's manufacturing industry is located in this area. Tobacco products, fertilizers, cloth and chemicals are produced in Piráeus.

HISTORY

THE DATE OF THE FIRST OLYMPIC GAMES was 776 B.C. For a long time, this was thought to be the beginning of Greek history. Although stories of older Greek civilizations are recounted in ancient Greek literature, much of it was thought to be mythological. Archeological digs, however, have unearthed treasures that represent times described in the Greek classics the *Iliad* and the *Odyssey*.

It is now known that two distinct civilizations flourished before the 5th century B.C., the time referred to as the Classical Greek Age. These were the Minoan and Mycenaean civilizations.

THE MINOAN CIVILIZATION Crete, the largest of the Greek islands, was home to this rich culture. Named after King Minos, one of the rulers of Crete, this civilization was a mighty but peaceful sea power that traded with people from Syria, Spain and Egypt, as well as mainland Greece.

The Minoans built beautiful cities and enjoyed many modern comforts at a time when people of other cultures were still living in caves. Archeologists have found that the palace at Knossos, a Minoan city in Crete, had an indoor plumbing system and other modern comforts.

The Minoan civilization came to an abrupt and mysterious end around 1400 B.C. By that time, the Greeks had already begun borrowing from the Minoans various aspects of their architecture and arts.

Opposite: **The Acropolis of Athens was built during the Golden Age of Greece. The Acropolis was actually a citadel built on the highest point of the city.**

Above: **The beautiful palace at Knossos, Crete, is nearly 3,500 years old. The reason for the decline of the Minoan civilization is still a mystery to archeologists.**

17

The most important city of the Mycenaean period was Mycenaé. The walls of this fortified city were made from stones so large that the later Greeks thought they were built by giants called "cyclops."

THE MYCENAEANS The early Mycenaeans migrated from Central Asia into Europe around 2000 B.C. and settled on the Peloponnesian peninsula.

Their civilization was as advanced as the Minoan. They built palaces with massive walls and were skilled artisans. The crafted daggers, shields, death masks and drinking cups which have been unearthed from Mycenaean ruins display their war-loving nature.

The *Iliad* chronicles a war between the Mycenaeans and the Trojans that began, according to legend, because Paris, the prince of Troy, kidnaped Helen, the wife of the king of Sparta. The long war ended with the capture of Troy. However, it is believed the strain of this lengthy war brought the collapse of the Mycenaean civilization around 1150 B.C.

This period is called the Heroic Age of Greece for the Greeks viewed the warring exploits of the Mycenaeans as courageous.

THE DARK AGES The downfall of the Mycenaeans was brought about by the Dorians, a tribe from northern Greece. The Dorians had new iron weapons which were superior to the bronze arms of the Mycenaeans.

The Dorian invasion marked the beginning of an era of instability that lasted until about 800 B.C. Farming was in a state of disorder, trade was almost nonexistent and there was a general decline in the arts. Thus, the period is known as the Dark Ages.

A period of colonial expansion occurred as a result of the growth of the city-state and the shortage of arable land. Grains and other crops grown in the settlements were sent back to Greece, and crops such as olives and wine grapes were used for trade. During this period, Greece was the maritime and commercial leader of the Mediterranean.

THE CITY-STATES AND CLASSICAL PERIOD

The rise of the city-state or *polis* as it was called, brought an end to the Dark Ages in 600 B.C. City-states developed after isolated villages banded together and grew into independent communities, each with its own system of government, industry, commerce and culture. Democracy in government first developed in the city-states, with every citizen taking turns to serve in the government, judiciary and the army. Some of the important city-states were Corinth, Athens, Thebes, Argos, Sparta, Aegina and Ephesus. This was the beginning of the Classical Period when Greece led the world in the arts and sciences.

But their development did not go unchallenged. Persia, a great empire in Asia Minor, longed to conquer Greece. King Darius of Persia waged a battle at Marathon for the city-state of Athens in 490 B.C., his large army outnumbering the Athenian defenders by about two to one. Nonetheless, the battle was a disaster for the Persians. Over six thousand Persian soldiers perished in the battle while the Greeks lost scarcely 200 men.

Ten years later, the Persians entered into naval battles with the Greeks at Salamis and Plataea. Greeks from all the city-states united under the leadership of Athens and successfully defeated the Persians at sea. The Persians were never to invade Greece again and, in the peace and security that followed, democracy and the arts flourished.

Above: **The Parthenon in Athens was the finest and largest temple on the Acropolis. Every four years, the ancient Greeks would hold a grand festival here to honor the goddess Athena, mythical founder of Athens.**

Opposite: **These graceful columns represent the Greek goddesses of Eréchtheion. Built in 395 B.C. the temple was used by the Crusaders as a church and by the Ottoman Turks as a mansion.**

THE GOLDEN AGE OF ATHENS

Athens emerged as the political and cultural center of Greece following the defeat of the Persians. The Athenian accomplishments in science, the arts, philosophy and architecture during this period were so advanced they greatly influenced later European civilizations.

Greek literature began during the Golden Age with the epic poems of Homer and Hesiod. To this day, people still watch the tragic Athenian plays and comedies of Sophocles, Euripides, Aeschylus and Aristophanes. The Parthenon and its exquisite sculptures were created during this period. This was the age of Socrates and his student Plato. They devoted their lives to the pursuit of truth and knowledge. Aristotle, Plato's student, was soon to make his contributions to science and knowledge.

Athenian supremacy was later challenged by Sparta, a rival city-state that had the support of other city-states. In 431 B.C., the destructive Peloponnesian War broke out and the conflict lasted for 27 years. It resulted in great disruptions to life and eventually, the downfall of Athens.

Sparta ruled Greece for a short period, but fighting continued with the other states and Sparta was defeated by Thebes. Thebes, too, was soon overthrown. Disunited, Greece was now vulnerable to invasions.

PERICLES

Pericles is possibly the most famous statesman who guided Athens. He was born to a noble family around 490 B.C. Pericles deeply believed in democracy and the rights of the ordinary citizen, and involved all citizens in the process of government. It was also under his leadership that the Parthenon and other temples were built.

Pericles established the Delian League, which was an alliance of city-states dedicated to the protection of one another. In 454 B.C., Athens seized the treasury of the Delian League and eventually all members of the league were forced to become part of the Athenian empire. Athens grew to be the center of Greek civilization and its cultural achievements.

The contributions of Pericles were so vital to the growth and prosperity of Athens that the time is also known as the "Golden Age of Pericles."

THE MACEDONIAN CONQUEST

By the middle of the 4th century B.C., King Phillip II of Macedonia in northern Greece, attacked the weakened city-states and ended Greek independence. He set out to unify the city-states under his rule. Phillip was a great admirer of Greek culture. His intention was to build a Greek-Macedonian army to conquer Persia and spread Greek civilization. However, Phillip was assassinated in 336 B.C. before realizing his goal.

Phillip's son, Alexander the Great, carried on his dreams and accomplished even greater things by conquering all of Persia and continuing on to India. Alexander's successful campaign created one of the largest empires of the ancient world.

Alexander ruled for only 13 years, dying in 323 B.C. His great empire broke up into many independent city-states and kingdoms. Among them were Syria, Egypt and Macedonia. But his legacy lived on in the city of Alexandria which became a center of learning, and some form of Greek culture survived in almost all the lands that he had conquered.

The phalanx is a solid, moving wall of men with shields and spears. Phillip II of Macedonia used this formation successfully in his campaign against the city-states.

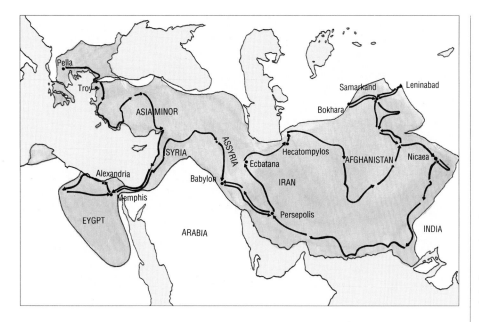

The Macedonian Empire of Alexander the Great. The arrows trace the route of Alexander in his 13-year campaign in which he amassed one of the largest empires of the ancient world.

THE ROMAN REPUBLIC

After Alexander, Macedonia continued to rule Greece for the next 200 years. Then, in 146 B.C., the Romans invaded and wrested the Greek Empire from the Macedonians. The Greek city-states welcomed the Romans, for they believed that the Roman Empire was the "protector of Greek freedom." The Greeks were given special treatment because of the Romans' great admiration for their intellectual and cultural life. Greece prospered once again and Greek culture continued to thrive.

Even Greek mythology and Greek gods formed the basis for Roman worship—until Christianity. Then, the Greeks became the first converts; Greek was the language of the Gospels. Many of the Christian martyrs were Greeks. Christianity was the force that reawakened Greek ideals.

In A.D. 285, Roman emperor Diocletian divided the Roman Empire into the western half, which was Latin-speaking, and the eastern half, which was Greek-speaking. He ruled the eastern part of the empire and appointed another emperor to watch over the western part. When Diocletian retired, a general named Constantine came to power in the east in A.D. 312. Within 12 years, Constantine gained control of the entire empire and officially moved the seat of power from the west to a city in

Art during the Byzantine era was greatly influenced by Christianity. Many inspiring works can be found in churches and monastries throughout Greece.

the Greek colony of Byzantium, which is now a part of Turkey. After his death, the city was renamed Constantinople in his honor.

For nearly 12 centuries, the city of Constantinople remained the capital of the Roman Empire, later known as the Byzantine Empire. The empire was Greek in culture and language; however, its laws and administration were completely Roman.

Justinian the Great (483–565) was the most famous emperor of the Byzantine Empire, known for expanding control eastward to Persia. He

This old abandoned Venetian fort is one of the many built during the time of the Crusades and the Holy Roman Empire.

was also responsible for codifying Roman law, which bears his name. All this time, Constantinople continued to flourish as a Greek cultural center.

FRANKISH AND VENETIAN OCCUPATION

The Byzantine Empire was torn apart by the fourth Crusade from Europe in 1204. Constantinople was plundered, and the Aegean Islands and the Greek mainland fell to the Frankish contingents and their Venetian allies.

Constantinople was freed some 55 years later, but much of Greece and the Aegean Islands remained under Frankish and Venetian occupation. Greece was divided into small states controlled by various Frankish and Venetian administrations.

By the mid-1400s, the Ottoman Turks were advancing. One by one the small Greek holdings fell to them. The recapture of Constantinople in 1453 was the beginning of Turkish domination of Greece and the end of the Byzantine Empire.

OTTOMAN RULE

Although the Turks were Moslems, they did permit religious freedom. The Greeks, therefore, found them less religiously offensive than the Roman Catholic Franks and Venetians—the Eastern Church had separated from papal authority in 1054. The Greeks soon realized, however, that Turkish rule was to isolate Greece and Greek culture and begin four centuries of oppression.

The Turks imposed heavy taxes, forced one of every five male Greek children to enlist in the Turkish army, killed groups of Greek men that they thought might lead a revolution, and engaged in numerous wars with Venice, using Greece as a battleground.

Though it caused poverty and hunger, oppression by the Turks strengthened Greek ethnic pride. Greek culture was preserved by the Church as the Turks allowed religious freedom. Soon, the Church, with its preservation of Greek language and history, came to represent Greek nationalism. Thus, the Church formed a close union with the people.

By the 1820s, the Ottoman Empire was losing its strength. The Greeks seized the opportunity to revolt in 1821. The battle was to last for more than 10 years, but by 1827, French, Russian and British forces joined the fight to free Greece.

The Turkish sultan finally signed the Treaty

of Adrianople in 1829 which allowed several Greek regions to form an independent state. This was accomplished in 1832. But there were still Greek islands and regions that remained under Turkish rule.

THE GREEK KINGDOM

The Treaty of London established a Greek kingdom made up of the mainland south of Thessaly, the Peloponnesus and the Euboea and Aegean Islands. The search for a monarch was begun and, finally, 17-year-old Prince Otho of Bavaria was named to the throne.

At first, Otho was popular with the people, but absolute control by the monarchy led to calls for a constitution and the eventual downfall of the king in 1862. Otho was replaced by Prince William of Denmark, and a new liberal and democratic constitution was enacted. Prince William was crowned King George I.

King George I reclaimed much of Greece's territory with the acquisition of the Ionian Islands from the British and Thessaly and southern Epirus from the Ottoman Empire. But a disastrous attempt to annex Crete from the Turks in 1897 resulted in war and subsequent defeat for Greece. But Greece never lost its dream of recovering its former lands. In 1912, the Balkan Wars erupted, allowing the victorious Greeks to regain Epirus, part of Macedonia and several islands, including Crete.

The beginning of the 20th century saw Greece in financial disarray, suffering from economic disorder and political unrest. King George I was assassinated in 1913 and Constantine was appointed to the throne. World War I saw Greece on the side of Germany, then, with the overthrow of Constantine, on the side of the Allies. King Alexander succeeded his father but died in 1920. Constantine returned to power amidst great rejoicing, but only two years later, he was blamed for the Greek defeat by

Opposite: **Christianity continued to be practiced in Byzantine monasteries as the Ottoman Moslems were tolerant of the people of the book—communities that believed in one God and had a written scripture, i.e. Jews and Christians.**

27

Below: **The Nazi swastika instilled fear and terror into people's hearts during World War II.**

Bottom: **The poster depicts the protest against the military dictatorship.**

MADE
IN
GREECE

1887-74

the Turks in Smyrna and was exiled again. For the next two years, King George II reigned until he was asked to leave. In 1925, a Greek republic was proclaimed.

The government faced many obstacles as many people still supported the monarchy. Finally, in 1935, George was called back to the throne. More political confusion resulted in the suspension of the constitution and a military dictator, Ioánnis Metaxas, ruled until Italy invaded Greece during World War II. The smaller Greek forces defeated the Italian army but were unable to hold off the German invasion and the subsequent occupation of Greece.

POST WORLD WAR II DEVELOPMENTS

German withdrawal in 1944 found the Greeks starving, without political leadership and their economy in ruins. In this confusion, the Communists in Greece tried to take over the country. Greece was torn by a civil war which lasted until 1949 with the defeat of the Communists.

The monarchy returned to power and the Greek economy improved with aid from the United States. A dispute arose in the 1950s with Turkey over Cyprus, a British colony with an 80% Greek population. After severe tensions, an agreement between Britain, Greece and Turkey resulted in independence for Cyprus in 1960.

Seven years later, a group of military colonels led by Colonel George Papadopoulos, overthrew the royal government. This group suspended important rights guaranteed by the constitution, outlawed political activity and replaced the leader of the Greek Orthodox Church. A new constitution was drawn up which provided for a stable government while eliminating political freedom and democracy.

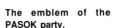

The emblem of the PASOK party.

DEMOCRACY RESTORED

In June of 1973, Papadopoulos proclaimed Greece a republic. He became president two months later, and announced plans for parliamentary elections. But in November of that year, another group of military officers overthrew the Papadopoulos government, making Lieutenant-General Phaidon Gizikis president.

Greece and Turkey came to blows again over Cyprus in 1974 when Greek forces landed on Cyprus and removed Archbishop Makarios from the presidency. Turkey sent troops to the island, but a full-scale war was averted by the signing of a ceasefire a few days later.

The military government collapsed in the face of the failed takeover of Cyprus and growing economic problems. Constantine Caramanlis, prime minister from 1956 to 1963, was recalled to head the new government in 1974. Parliamentary elections were held in November of that year, followed in December by a vote to make the country a republic.

From 1981 through 1989, the Panhellenic Socialist Movement (PASOK) had control of parliament. Andreas Papandreou became prime minister. The New Democratic Party took control of the government after the April 1990 elections with Constantine Mitsotakis as prime minister.

GOVERNMENT

GREECE HAS BEEN A DEMOCRATIC REPUBLIC since 1974. At that time, a new constitution was put into effect that clearly spells out guarantees of civil liberties and individual rights. The great care taken in ensuring these privileges is probably the result of experiences under the oppressive military dictatorship.

The president is the head of state and is elected for a five-year term by parliament. The powers of the president are mainly ceremonial. Unlike in the United States, the president is not elected by the people. This ensures that the political majority in parliament will be unchallenged in the decisions it makes. The parliament, which is called the Vouli, is composed of 300 deputies who hold office for four years. Parliament is elected by the people. The head of the majority party in the parliament is appointed the prime minister.

INDEPENDENCE TO WORLD WAR II

Although Greece is the birthplace of democracy, over the centuries many of its governments have been undemocratic. It is sometimes said that the Greek civilization has been around for so long that it has had a chance to try nearly every form of government!

For a short period of time after gaining independence in the 1830s, Greece was a republic. However, many nationals had divided into opposing parties during the fight for freedom, and the formation of a new government did not unite these factions. Because of this turmoil, it was decided that a monarchy would be a more effective system of government. Bavaria's Prince Otho was selected as the new king.

In an attempt to curb the absolute power of the king, a revolt in 1844 led to the adoption of a constitution that set up a two-house legislative body.

The birthplace of democracy, Greece has also experienced much tyranny in modern times.

Opposite: **A Greek** *evzone* **or soldier in traditional uniform stands guard in front of the presidential palace.**

The Parliament Building stands in front of Constitution Square in Athens. In the evening, the square is filled with people taking a stroll or simply enjoying the view.

The king's powers were not diminished by these actions and by 1862, discontent led to a second revolt which deposed Otho. The new liberal and democratic constitution of 1864 established a new monarchy. Prince William of Denmark was crowned King George I. The constitution also called for the creation of a unicameral (one-house) legislature based on representation by vote and very limited powers for the king.

In the years between the 1860s and 1952, parliament reverted to a two-house body and then back again to a one-house body. A new constitution set forth in 1952 was very similar in principle to the constitution of 1864 and currently remains in effect.

MILITARY DICTATORSHIP

After 1947, however, there was strong military involvement in politics. This resulted in political instability. From 1954 to 1963, the key political figure in Greece was the prime minister, Constantine Caramanlis. He tried to strengthen the country's ties with Western Europe by establishing links with the European Economic Community, which was finally realized many years later.

These guards are doing the "goose-step" in front of the Tomb of the Unknown Soldier.

Throughout the early 1960s, Georgios Papandreou, an important social reformer, and the Center Union Party were instrumental in creating an era of considerable unrest. After years of riots, strikes and political fighting, the military stepped in to take full control in May 1967. The king tried to regain power by means of a coup. This unsuccessful attempt resulted in King Constantine II having to flee the country. The military dictatorship lasted for seven years.

This dictatorship created an era that is remembered for its cruelty. Greece became a military country in which dissenters were persecuted, often by brutal means.

An ill-fated attempt by the Greek military to overthrow the government of the nearby island of Cyprus caused the downfall of the dictatorship. The coup attempt provoked the Turkish government to send in troops, which brought Greece on the brink of war with its neighbor and long-time enemy. Greek senior officers abandoned their support for the ruling colonel and called for the former prime minister to return from exile. It was time for democracy to return to its country of birth. A new constitution went into effect in June 1975 that abolished the monarchy and established a republic.

The architecture of this government building is modeled after the buildings of ancient Greece. Many Greeks hope that future governments will also retain the democratic values that had made ancient Greece so great and powerful.

DEMOCRACY RETURNS

The Panhellenic Socialist Movement (PASOK) is one of the strongest political parties in Greece. It formed the government of Greece for most of the 1980s. Many changes have benefited the Greek people since then. Women have acquired equal rights, the voting age was lowered to 18 and civil marriage was legalized. A very positive change in the Greek political scene has been made—the military is now involved solely in defense matters and is no longer a part of the political process.

PASOK's popularity has grown consistently since its founding in 1974. In its first election, 14% of the voters supported the party. PASOK rose in popularity until it captured 48% of the votes in 1985. As is typical of Greek style, political parties are closely associated with the personality of a strong leader. In the case of PASOK, Andreas Papandreou was the driving force. He has been a key figure in Greek politics for most of his adult life. Papandreou was appointed prime minister in 1981 and remained in that position until 1989, when PASOK lost the majority in parliament. This loss was partly due to a drop of voter confidence in Papandreou as a result of his personal and financial difficulties.

The parliamentary elections in April 1990 turned the majority over to the New Democracy Party under the leadership of Constantine Mitsotakis.

ARMED FORCES

Greece is protected by an army, an air force and a navy. Greek men must serve two years in one of these armed forces. Although all nations understand the importance of maintaining national security by having a strong military, the situation is a bit more complicated for Greece. Though it is believed that there is a constant danger of war with Turkey, the Greeks are mindful that a military coup overthrew the Greek government as recently as 25 years ago. The Hellenic Republic is working to maintain a delicate balance to sustain effective but loyal armed forces.

CYPRUS

A special challenge for the Greek government is the island of Cyprus. Because it was divided as a result of hostilities in 1974, Cyprus is protected in its southern half by Greek troops, and the northern half is protected by Turkish forces.

The constitution of Cyprus specifies that the vice-president of the republic and 10 cabinet ministers must be Turkish, while 70% of the House of Representatives is composed of elected Greek officials, chosen from the Greek community. Turkish representatives, the remaining 30% of the legislative body, are similarly elected from the Turkish community. The two communities are self-governing with regard to education, culture and religion. All matters pertaining to government fall under the jurisdiction of the joint administration.

ECONOMY

GREECE IS MAINLY AN AGRICULTURAL COUNTRY whose economy was nearly destroyed during World War II. Industries that had been developed after World War I were in ruins by the late 1940s.

There have been notable improvements in the economy since the 1950s and, from the mid-60s through the mid-70s, it experienced an annual growth rate of 10%. Personal spending increased tremendously and the standard of living improved.

In 1981, Greece became the 10th member of the European Community (EC), which is a group of Western European nations that try to unite their resources into one strong economy. However, Greece remains one of the poorest countries in Western Europe. In fact, world economic organizations characterize Greece as a "newly industrializing country," which puts it in the same category as countries like Mexico and other developing nations.

Its membership in the EC, while providing tremendous advantages for expanding and bolstering the economy, points out the unusual character of Greece. Though Greece is a European country by virtue of its people, it is not necessarily comparable to other Western European economies. Greece is geographically isolated from Western Europe and very Mediterranean in culture. Nonetheless, the Greeks would like to be a part of the Western European way of life.

The scarcity of natural resources and arable farmland, paired with its relatively young manufacturing sector, are the major contributors to Greece's slower economic life. The brightest spot on the country's economic horizon is tourism.

Opposite: **Water taxis in the harbor. Most industries of the Greek economy from fishing to shipping are dependent on the sea.**

Above: **The dry and arid climate of Greece is ideal for the cultivation of cotton.**

Tourism is one of the biggest industries in Greece. Tourists patronize restaurants, hotels, taxis and help the growth of many other local businesses.

TOURISM

Since the 1970s, tourism has been the biggest growth sector in the country, outperforming all other areas. Beautiful island beaches, plentiful sunshine, breathtaking ancient ruins and Greece's well-deserved reputation for hospitality have made it a favorite vacation spot. More than 8.5 million tourists visited Greece in 1989 alone—that's about 80% of the country's entire population!

The tourist industry has its share of problems too. First of all, the islands and Athens are the favorite vacation spots, so during peak vacation times those areas become uncomfortably crowded. And because tourism is seasonal, there are periods of time when facilities remain unused. Greece's proximity to the Arab world and the recent terrorist activities associated with these countries have also had a negative impact on the tourist industry.

These young tobacco plants form the backbone of one of the main export industries of Greece. Most of the tobacco will be sold to Europe.

AGRICULTURE

Agriculture employs approximately 30% of the work force and crops are grown on approximately 30% of the total land area. Greece has the lowest proportion of forest land among all the EC countries.

Wheat covers more crop land than any other commodity, followed by cotton, tobacco, vegetables and other grains. Also grown are grapes, olives, lemons and other fruits.

Livestock is raised on pastures and meadows, which amount to 40% of the land. However, Greek livestock is of such inferior quality that animals from other countries are imported to breed with local cattle, sheep and goats to improve the quality of the animals. Until this program is successful, Greece will continue to import meat and dairy products.

The average farm size is only eight acres, and the harvest is usually just enough to feed a family without any surplus for sale. This is largely due to outdated farming techniques. The government has stepped in to teach more modern techniques and foster the idea of specialized farming. In this way, it hopes to grow enough for export to other countries.

Apart from crops like grapes and olives, Greece's dry summers and lack of fertile soil continue to prevent agriculture from contributing more than 6% of the Gross National Product.

OLIVES

Greece is the world's third leading producer of olives. Olive trees flourish in Greece because they thrive in the dry climate. It was believed that the olive was a gift of the goddess Athena to Athens and that, through its cultivation, the people became prosperous. The largest plantations are found in Delphi and on the island of Euboea.

Farmers prune their trees in the spring, using the trimmings as fuel. Several weeks later, small white flowers appear before transforming into the familiar hard green fruit. Later in the season, families go out with long poles to knock the green olives down. These olives are usually exported. The ripe black olives available later in the season are preferred by the Greeks.

Hundreds of types of olive trees, which are often quite old with gnarled branches and trunks, are grown for two types of olives: those for eating and those produced for making oil. The majority of olive trees produce oil-olives.

The black olive harvest officially begins in November. Sheets are spread beneath the trees and pickers on ladders run their hands over the loaded branches. The ripe fruit falls to the sheets, leaving the not-yet-ready olives on the branches to mature. Several weeks later, the procedure is repeated and this continues periodically throughout winter. The harvest is usually completed in February.

Eating-olives are usually pickled in barrels of brine. Oil-olives are sometimes crushed immediately after picking for home use; many villages own several olive presses for extracting the oil. Most other olives are sold to food processing companies.

The harvest from the seas around Greece is rich and plentiful because the warm waters encourage the growth of the basic fish food—plankton.

FISHING

Fishing and diving for sponges are major occupations of the islanders. Greeks have been involved with the sea since ancient times and more than 50,000 persons continue to make a living from it. They are employed to process and can the fish either at the ports or on the thousands of fishing boats.

The Aegean Sea is remarkably rich in fish. Local fishing boats pull in bass, lobster, cod, red mullet, swordfish, perch, carp, mackerel and prawns. In all, nearly 250 species of fish are found in Greek waters. Nonetheless, Greece still imports many fish products.

Sponge fishing is a specialty of many islanders. Because many years of harvesting have depleted some areas, divers now go into deeper, more dangerous waters. The sponge harvest is cleaned only minimally at sea. The covering membrane is torn off to prevent decay, but the final cleaning, which includes trimming, drying and grading, is done at the port.

SAILING THE SEVEN SEAS

Shipping is a vital part of the Greek economy, providing more than 100,000 jobs. Greece's merchant fleet is the largest in the world and makes up 70% of the EC's total fleet. Many Greek businessmen of humble beginnings have made fortunes by amassing a shipping fleet.

However, there are serious drawbacks to this livelihood. Whenever the world experiences a recession, many ships lie idle. Likewise, pleasure cruise liners, a part of the tourist industry as well as the shipping industry, are affected by economic downturns as well as world events.

Another difficulty lies in finding enough people to man the fleets. The lonely life of a seaman has become less attractive in recent decades, and because 75% of a ship's crew must be Greek according to Greek law, ship owners must provide excellent benefits and pay very high salaries to attract enough personnel. Even recruiting the remaining crew members has become an increasing challenge.

An important aspect of the Greek shipping industry is that it has enabled the country to compete in the world market in spite of its less developed economy.

INDUSTRY

Industrialization has come slowly to Greece. However, since World War II, there has been a determined effort to mechanize industry. Government policies have supported the growth of new industries such as food processing.

Factories have been built mostly on the outskirts of Thessaloníki and Athens. Principal manufactured products are cement, cigarettes, clothing, processed foods and textiles.

Historically, the Greek manufacturing industry has developed out of small artisan businesses. There are still a great number of business concerns or cottage industries that have fewer than 10 employees and depend on labor more than equipment to produce goods such as textiles, clothing and footwear. Their efforts account for about one-fifth of the country's economic production.

The Greek national carrier is Olympic Airways. Air transportation helps the economy by making it easier to export goods and by ferrying tourists to and from the country.

This old man is a stone mason. In the tradition of the old Athenian artists, he breaks the stones and creates sculptures for decorating homes.

MINING

Although Greece has a good variety of mineral deposits, the supply is limited. In the 1980s, more than 22,000 workers were employed in mining. With the exception of lignite, which is a brownish-black coal, and bauxite, which is the principal source of aluminum, most other Greek mines operate below their productive capacity.

About 90% of mined lignite is used to generate electricity. It is found mainly on the island of Euboea, central Peloponnesus and in the Ptolemais basin in the Pindus Mountains.

Other minerals found in Greece include chromite, zinc, lead, copper, asbestos and magnesite. In the 1980s, mining represented only 1.3% of the Gross National Product.

THE EUROPEAN COMMUNITY (EUROPEAN ECONOMIC COMMUNITY)

The ravages of World War II had so devastated Europe that a movement was begun to organize the countries of Europe economically.

In 1951, Belgium, France, West Germany, Luxembourg and the Netherlands formed the European Economic Community (EEC), which is also known as the Common Market. Recently, the EEC has changed its name to European Community (EC) to reflect the greater political and social amalgamation among member countries.

The goal of the Common Market is to combine the member countries' total economic resources into a union where all tariffs (taxes on imported goods) and quotas would be canceled and a single tariff would be established on all imported goods. In the 12- to 15-year period that was needed to accomplish this, the Common Market allowed free movement of capital and labor and enacted common policies for transport, foreign trade and agriculture.

The idea has proved very successful. With a combined population of 160 million, the union produces one-seventh of the world's coal, automobiles and electricity and one-fifth of its steel. This new organization has become a powerful force in the world economy.

The smaller members of the EC really benefited from this arrangement. For instance, a small country like Belgium is able to sell its products in a market of 160 million consumers. Previously, tariffs added to goods sold outside Belgium made them too costly to compete with home-made products. Under the EC's economic policy, trade between member countries is as simple as selling a Detroit-made automobile in Florida.

Several other features characterize the successful EC venture:

• It has created a general tariff on imports for all its member countries, allowing all EC nations to be protected from foreign competition.

• Each country has been able to reduce the number of products it produces, allowing it to concentrate on what it does best.

• Member countries have expanded their overseas trade, because the agreement included markets that were controlled by member countries. For example, at the time of the EC's formation, Algeria was a French colony, and Western European nations were then able to trade with Algeria for the first time.

By 1972, the very successful Common Market expanded to include Denmark, Ireland and Great Britain. Greece joined the league in 1981, and Portugal and Spain in 1986.

GREEKS

THE POPULATION OF GREECE is nearly homogeneous, or uniformly Greek. In fact, about 98% of the people are Greek. The remaining 2% is composed of Turks, Vlachs, Slavs, Albanians, Jews and Gypsies. Because members of these groups have distinct religions and often speak languages other than Greek, they are regarded as outsiders.

Like all ethnic groups, the Greeks have personality traits that are admirable and others that are less attractive. But the local people

have an explanation for that. They feel that the noble blood of their ancient Greek ancestors runs through their veins, as does the blood of the "barbarians" who later ruled their land.

According to the Greeks, the courageous, creative side of the Greek personality is their Hellenic heritage. Jealousy, obstinacy, selfishness and other faults are the Romanic side, inherited from the many years of Roman domination.

Today, the Romanic personality within the Greeks is considered to be the practical side that focuses on reality, makes decisions on matters concerning money and power, bypasses rules to achieve goals, values education and loves the native region and its folk music and dance.

The Hellenic side regards matters in non-material terms, reaches for ideals, respects and adheres to the law, relies on logic for making decisions and for advancement, and prefers European dance and music.

Opposite: **Two of the nicest things about Greece are the warm hospitality of its people and the architecture of the pretty towns in which they live.**

Above: **The people of Greece are hardworking and many continue to ply their trade till a ripe old age.**

47

Schoolchildren on a beach. Soon, many of these children will look beyond their country's borders for work in the European Community or other foreign lands.

POPULATION TRENDS

When repression ended in the mid-1970s with the overthrow of the military junta, the people of Greece began migrating to the cities. Today, Athens alone is home to more than 30% of the population. At the same time, one-third of the population still live in rural areas and farm for a living. For them, the land and its climate are still important to their lives.

Because the land is mostly unsuitable for farming and quite rugged, and because of centuries of persecution, war and poverty, many people have left Greece to settle in other countries. From the end of the 19th century through the end of World War II, Greeks have emigrated in great numbers to the United States, Canada and Australia. In recent decades, especially since Greece joined the European Community, Greeks have been migrating to Western Europe (particularly West Germany), joining other Europeans to meet the labor needs of the more industrialized countries.

However, no matter what country Greek emigrants have adopted, they continue to be citizens of Greece, both by law and in their hearts.

MINORITY GROUPS

Greece's ethnic make-up has not always been so uniform. During the centuries of Turkish dominance, people of different ethnic groups and nationalities from all over the Ottoman Empire settled in Greece. In the 160 years since Greece attained independence, the citizenry has gradually returned to an overwhelming majority of those with Greek ancestry. Nonetheless, several interesting groups comprise the 2% of non-Greek inhabitants.

An old Turkish fort in the town of Ioaninna in Epirus is all that is left from the many centuries of Ottoman rule. Many Turks have returned to their country following the independence of Greece.

TURKS   The treaty that ended the Greco-Turkish War in the 1920s specified details of an exchange of Greek and Turkish nationals. As a result, 400,000 Turks living in Greece returned to their homeland while nearly triple that number of Greeks returned to Greece. However, there were some exemptions: Turks living in Thrace, the northeastern area of Greece that borders Turkey, did not have to comply with the exchange. This region remains home to a Turkish minority numbering approximately 100,000. Similarly, Greeks living in Istanbul were not required to leave if they preferred to remain.

Many towns in Thrace have Turkish majorities and their local governments are run by Moslem officials. Children of this region attend schools where the language of instruction is Turkish and several Turkish language newspapers are published there. Despite ongoing friction between Turkey and Greece, especially in Cyprus, the inhabitants of Thrace generally coexist peacefully.

Many Vlachs in Greece work as shepherds. Shepherds are recognizable by the crook and staff which they use to herd their sheep.

VLACHS In reality, Vlachs are not an ethnic group. The term is actually used by Greek villagers to identify those who pursue shepherding as an occupation. Because members of the Aromani and Koutsovlach ethnic minorities are by tradition shepherds in Greece, the term Vlach has been used to refer to them as an ethnic group.

Vlachs, who only recently have been estimated to number 100,000, speak a Romanian dialect in addition to speaking Greek. The majority of them worship in the Greek Orthodox Church.

Another group of shepherds, the Sarakatsani, are often mistaken for Vlachs. This group, however, speaks only Greek and has entirely different values and social structures from the Vlachs. The two groups are quite competitive because they share identical trades and must vie for the same plots of grazing land for their roaming herds.

SLAVS The Slavs of Greece can be divided into two groups: the Macedo-Slavs from Macedonia and the Pomaks from Thrace. Inhabitants of Greece for centuries, Macedo-Slavs are the descendants of ancient Slavic migrants who continue to speak Slavic languages. The Bulgarian-speaking Pomaks are Moslems who were also not required to participate in the population exchanges of the 1920s. The Slav ethnic group is estimated at about 60,000.

ALBANIANS Most Greeks of Albanian descent no longer strive to maintain cultural traditions as they once did. As recently as 50 years ago, it would have been possible to encounter numerous villages where residents spoke only Albanian. Even in the 1970s, some elderly Albanians in Greece spoke no Greek. Today, however, most inhabitants of Albanian descent

consider themselves to be Greek and are affiliated with the Greek Orthodox Church. Generally, Albanian Greeks live in Attica and Boetia, the Peloponnesus and on some Aegean islands. There is also a small community of Greek-speaking Moslems of Albanian descent near the Greek border with Albania.

This Greek woman is selling traditional crochet shawls and tablecloths. Though Greece has faced many difficult moments in its history, its people have managed to preserve their culture and keep alive their Hellenic identity.

JEWS Thessaloníki is the historical center of Jewish intellectual and commercial life, but there are other Jewish communities in Thessaly, Macedonia and Epirus. There have been Jews in Greece since before the time of Christ. As far back as the 13th century, Jewish immigrants from Italy, France, Germany and Poland settled in Thessaloníki. The greatest influx, however, was in the 15th century when the Jews, expelled from Spain during the Inquisition, were lured to Greece because of religious tolerance under Turkish rule.

They landed in Thessaloníki and brought traditions and a culture that resulted in civic and commercial improvements. The Jews developed trade and schools there, and the area became known throughout the Middle East and Europe as a cultural and business center. Ladino, a modified Spanish spoken by the relocated Jews, is still spoken by some in Greece's Jewish community today.

Prior to World War II, there were approximately 76,000 Jews in Greece, a population that diminished to fewer than 16,000 by the end of the war. Many Greek Jews died as victims of Nazi genocide or fled to Athens or to the mountains to hide. Today's Jewish population mainly works in trade or as professionals.

GYPSIES: CITIZENS OF THE WORLD

Gypsies are a wandering, close-knit people who are found throughout Europe, including Greece. They move from town to town telling fortunes, performing with animals, playing their distinctive music on flutes and fiddles, and doing odd jobs that allow them to maintain their traveling lifestyle. In Greece, they are found mainly in the northern and central parts of the country, working as tinsmiths and dealing in ironware. Because they are always on the move, there are no precise population figures for Gypsies in Greece or in any other country.

The language of the Gypsies is Romany and it is through recent detailed linguistic study of Romany that the origin of this ethnic group has been traced. The name "Gypsy" was given to these people because it was originally thought they had migrated to Europe from Egypt. However, careful examination of the Romany language has shown that the Gypsies originated in India, for the features it shares with Sanskrit (the classical language of India) and other Indian languages are striking.

Interestingly, loan words also create a type of atlas that depicts the general path the Gypsies followed after migrating westward into Europe in about A.D. 1000. Vocabulary and word forms show that they first went to Afghanistan and later Iran (then Persia). Some groups traveled on to North Africa and Syria while others proceeded to Greece and then crossed the Balkans. Gypsies first arrived on Mount Athos in the 12th century and other groups reached Crete and Corfu by the 14th century. The Gypsies' stay in Greece since that time has resulted in many Greek words being assimilated into Romany.

Because of their unfamiliar customs, traditions and dark physical appearance, Gypsies have always faced hostility, discrimination and sometimes persecution. They are accepted by many rural Greeks and even welcomed by some as temporary farm hands during the olive and grain harvests. However, many older superstitious villagers hate and fear Gypsies because they believe that the Gypsies made the nails for the cross on which Jesus Christ was crucified.

Rich or poor, many Greeks have flat, open sunroofs on their houses for rest and leisure. Wealthier houses such as this one have roofs decorated with tiles and furnished with deck chairs.

SOCIAL DIVISIONS

There are no rigid class lines in Greece and social mobility is quite attainable. In general, Greeks are able to climb up the social ladder through higher education or property ownership.

In villages, the lowest layer is composed of farm laborers who own no land, the mentally disabled and the emotionally disturbed. A middle level is made up of smaller farm owners, merchants and skilled workers. Prosperous farm owners, large shopkeepers and very successful merchants, professionals and government officials make up the upper level. While land ownership remains important, education is the sure route to improve one's social status.

In towns and urban centers, the lowest class is made up of people who are uneducated, own no property and have little money. Generally, these individuals are laborers, unskilled factory workers and servants. The middle category actually consists of two divisions, the lower of which encompasses craftsmen, smaller shopkeepers and merchants, and civil servants. The higher-middle class is made up of professionals, executives, small businessmen and senior officials. The Greek urban upper class consists of ship owners, bankers, big merchants, industrialists and highly successful professionals.

FOLK COSTUMES

Each province in Greece has a traditional costume that is worn only on festive occasions. Patterns and styles reflect all periods of Greek history, but generally have one thing in common: the fabric is of high quality and contains exquisite and sometimes elaborate embroidery. Greek women have excelled at embroidery for centuries.

One effect of the nation's drive towards urbanization is the feeling villagers have that anything produced in the city or elsewhere in Europe is superior to local craftsmanship. Everyday clothing that used to be made in the villages has been replaced with machine-made shirts and suits for men and inexpensive cotton dresses for women regardless of quality.

A traditional folk costume that is used year-round is the *foustanella* worn by the elite Greek Palace Guards. On ceremonial occasions these sentries wear full-white shirt and skirt, an embroidered dark blue short jacket, white woolen stockings and red shoes with a large black pom-pom on the toes. A colorful hat tops the whole outfit.

LIFESTYLE

GREEKS EMBRACE THE IDEOLOGY of Hellenism which is a collection of all the ideals which were exceptional and glorious in ancient Greece. All Greeks, regardless of background, occupation or town, are aware of the tremendous role their ancestors played in the development of Western civilization. During the years of Ottoman rule, Greeks relied on Hellenism to retain their identity and to stoke the flames of nationalism. This spirit continues to live within them today as modern Greeks see in their life and culture something that they can offer to the world.

ALL IN THE FAMILY

The basic household in Greece consists of the husband, wife, unmarried children and, quite often, the grandparents. In the cities, it is also common to have other relatives living in the same household. Unmarried adult children rarely live outside of their parents' home and, in some regions, it is customary for married children to reside with parents until they have established their own households.

Traditionally, a rural newlywed couple will return to the home of the groom's parents or to a residence provided for them in the village. This extended family living arrangement may continue indefinitely, especially when labor is needed for the family farm. On some of the islands, it is the custom for the married couple to live in the wife's village and often, it is her family that will provide the home as part of the dowry.

Family members in Greek homes have established roles; all work together to preserve the family property. In poorer families which have no property, the sons contribute their wages. The child's duty is to share his or her home with the parents for as long as they live. As a result, few senior citizens live alone in Greece and fewer reside in old folks' homes.

A common religion, a great heritage, and a common popular tongue tend to make all Greeks feel as one people. Combined with this sense of unity, is the interest in, and appetite for, political discussion.

Opposite: **A modern city center in Crete. This century has brought much economic change to Greece. However, there are still many rural areas in Greece that remain underdeveloped.**

Much trust and reliance are placed in friends and working partners. In Greece they are regarded as a form of extended family.

THE GODFATHER

Relationships between families that are not related are often created by the selection of a *koumbaros* ("koom-BAH-ros"). This individual is the godparent at a baptism or a sponsor at a wedding. The *koumbaros* is like a member of the family in this spiritual kinship. Often the sponsor of a wedding couple will be the godparent of the couple's first child.

Though it is an artificially created kinship, religious law prohibits marriage between godchildren and the children of a *koumbaros* because the relationship between the family and the godparent represents such an important family linkage.

PATRIDA

Greeks not only maintain close ties with an extended family of parents, godparents, uncles and aunts, but they also feel a strong obligation to their native village, district or province. When meeting fellow Greeks, people will try to determine whether they come from the same region or if they have any relatives that stay in that region. This way, Greeks will create a type of kinship with non-relatives when they are away from home. This devotion to one's home is called *patrida*.

PATRONAGE

Because Greeks are intensely loyal to their family, they often feel that the world of non-relatives is a hostile place, and that they will not get fair treatment from non-family members, especially government officials.

This widespread belief has created a heavy reliance on patrons. A network of patrons bypasses "red tape" and allows the client to achieve his goals. It is a clear give-and-take relationship which serves both the patron and the client equally. For example, in addition to pledging loyalty and political support, a fisherman can offer a weekly fresh catch to the patron in return for a favor such as obtaining a passport. An artificial kinship is created via this process, and a lifetime relationship is established.

These men have gathered at a *kafeneíon* for drinks and companionship.

PHILOXENIA

Greek hospitality, or *philoxenia*, is part of a long tradition. Some say it began in Homeric times as a sacred duty; others feel that the cruelty of the land itself caused Greeks to accept with open arms any soul that has been at the mercy of the terrain.

Whatever its origin, it is clear that the stranger benefits from the respect the Greeks have for the wants and needs of others. The Greeks judge themselves by the extent of their hospitality. Should they fail in their duty to put their guests' needs before their own, it is considered a black mark against their ancestors and community as a whole.

OF MEN AND WOMEN

Woman washing clothes. In many Greek households, it is still the duty of the wife to look after the home while the men go out to work.

The Greeks have very fixed ideas about the differences in sexuality and personality of men and women. Traditional thinking holds that women are emotional, vulnerable and less disciplined than men. However, these characteristics are not necessarily negative. They are the perfect complement to the qualities of men, for it is believed that the male-female relationship is that of two dissimilar creatures living together in a mutually beneficial bond.

Marriage is an ideal in Greek society, but it is not seen as the culmination of a love affair. Rather, through marriage a woman sets up a home in which she can care for her husband and produce a family, which will ideally include a son. A man perpetuates his family line through marriage. Traditional marriages are based on mutual dependence and understanding and are often the result of an arrangement rather than American-style courtship and dating.

Greek women are raised to pamper men. Utmost respect is shown to men in public. At a dinner gathering, women will prepare plates for their husbands and be sure that the men's needs are met before they consider their own. At social events, men and women separate almost immediately, and often the activity of choice for females will be preparing food while men socialize.

Marriage and family are the prime focus of life for Greek women, and they measure their worth by their accomplishments as mothers and homemakers. A traditional Greek wife is the symbol of her husband's honor, and her exemplary behavior is a requirement. This has been the way of life for centuries: Euripides, an ancient Greek dramatist, wrote that "a woman should be everything in the house and nothing outside it."

Every member of the family helps out in the family business whether it is fishing, farming or manufacturing.

This apparent male domination does not necessarily leave women powerless. Because Greek women have complete control over the running of the household and the raising of the children, their weakness is power; complaints and tears are sometimes as effective as demands. And many women have a strong sense of worth and importance within the framework of the Greek male-female relationship.

Greek men are considered the protectors of their families, responsible for both honor and material goods. They are expected to appear to adhere to the highest standards at all times, and this is also what Greek men expect of their wives and children.

A Greek husband is responsible for disciplining his children, but little, if any, childcare. He is a dominating, powerful figure from whom boys develop their sexual identity. The man does, however, consider his family and home the center of his life. He views his work as a means of providing for the family, but not necessarily as a source of fulfillment. The importance of the father within the family structure can be seen in the naming ritual to which Greeks adhere: the first son is named after his father's father. If a second son is born, the mother may then name him after her father.

difference

Old man and his donkey. Donkeys are still common modes of transport for farmers and people who live in the mountains and other rugged terrain.

PHILOTIMO

A key social value in the lives of the Greeks is one called *philotimo*. It is about gaining respect from others by maintaining one's self-esteem. This value serves as a code of ethics that tempers the daily behavior of all Greeks. Boys grow up with the knowledge that they must never disgrace the family honor and be ever-ready to defend it. Girls know that obedience is essential, and as they grow older they realize that their chastity and purity is a symbol of their family's honor.

This characteristic is one that is not only revered by members of all classes, but expected of them. The importance of public honor is so sacred that, as recently as a decade ago, a typical defense in most murder cases was that the crime was committed to uphold the family honor!

EDUCATION

Formal education is greatly valued and is seen as an important factor in moving up the social ladder. The education system has undergone reform in the last 20 years, making it more accessible and more practical. Students who pass the university entrance exams do not pay for tuition, room and board, or books. But because Greece is a male-dominated country, for many years rural families believed that school was not necessary for females. A great number of Greece's illiterates are therefore women.

AMONG FRIENDS

Greeks love to socialize and prefer to be among friends. During warm weather months, families go out nightly and on Sunday afternoons for walks. Father leads the way, keeping several steps ahead, while Mother and the children follow respectfully behind. Along the way, families will stop and visit other families; parents may sit on benches while the children run around the village square.

The Greeks love to talk; they love poetry, arguing about politics, and word play. They would rather pass time at a crowded beach or park than take a short trip to get some peace and quiet. They prefer to travel around cities and villages in groups of friends.

After an evening jaunt the Greek father will often stop at the local *kafeneíon* ("kah-FAYN-ay-on"), which is a coffeehouse. His wife and children will continue on home, while the man of the house fingers his worry beads and discusses world events over a cup of coffee or a glass of wine. Coffeehouses are almost totally patronized by men.

Strolling along Syntagma Square in Athens. It is a popular place to meet friends and to drink coffee at the many outdoor cafes.

WORRY BEADS

A traditional aspect of *kafeneíon* life is the clicking of worry beads. It creates a type of background music for the spirited banter of the café. Greek men have been manipulating these beads for centuries; the activity occupies their hands and helps while away the time.

Contrary to their name, worry beads or *komboloia* ("kahm-BOH-loy-ah"), have little to do with worry. In fact, they are said to lessen tension and the manipulation of these beads has been referred to as the oldest and simplest way to relieve stress.

Though it is hard to trace the origins of worry beads, it is believed that beads may have been first used in India by Hindus and Buddhists as prayer beads. Later, the Moslem world began using them as worry and prayer beads, often with 99 beads per string to honor the number of ways Allah can be glorified in the Koran. It is therefore thought that the Greeks adopted the use of worry beads from the Turks.

LOVE IS IN THE AIR

Until recently in Greece, dating was not just a matter of interest for the two young persons involved. Traditionally it was an experience that concerned the nuclear family—parents, brothers, sisters and any other relative who cared to get involved. Single people did not choose whom they would marry; this was arranged by the parents of the prospective bride and groom. Though this seldom occurs in modern-day Greece, parental approval is still of great importance.

In the cities, it is common for couples to show affection in public. In the villages and smaller towns, people are much more traditional and such behavior is frowned upon.

The concept of honor emerges strongly in dating and courtship. In courtship, honor is the display of the traditional qualities that differentiate the roles of men and women. Young men must appear manly, while women must display modesty.

As recently as 25 years ago, young unmarried women dressed to conceal their sexual attributes. It was essential to show the family's honor by displaying absolute innocence and modesty. Today's young Greek women, however, dress in the latest styles and need not maintain an air of naïveté. Nonetheless, many women still do not spend time alone with a man until they are formally engaged; a hint of flirtation on the part of a woman would result in great condemnation.

While premarital chastity is still the ideal, only the appearance of chastity is crucial. Great care is taken to present a prospective bride as virtuous, particularly in the village communities. On the other hand young men, especially in the cities, often maintain their "manly honor" by having premarital sex with several partners.

Marriage is always a family affair in Greece and would not be complete without a reunion and a big, but simple, celebration.

TYING THE KNOT

Civil marriages have been legal since 1982, but most Greek couples see the church ceremony as the only valid contract. Traditionally, a church wedding symbolizes the formation of the family.

An honored tradition in Greece is that of the *proika*, or dowry. Throughout the ages, Greek women have entered marriage with a piece of property or a sum of money given to them by their parents. It is intended to help a young couple become established in their new life together. The father is responsible for accumulating the *proika*.

The *proika* is often used as a means for upward social mobility, and family honor is closely associated with providing an ample dowry. A young woman with a significant dowry stands a very good chance of attracting a husband of higher social standing. Her marriage and new-found status will, in turn, help her siblings in finding suitable partners.

The value of the *proika* is determined by family status and by the personal attributes of the bride and groom. For example, a more valuable dowry will be required of a woman who is marrying into a family of higher social rank.

Recent strides in equality among the sexes have resulted in the dowry no longer being required. As sexual equality becomes more prevalent in Greek society, women are finding that a career can serve as the equivalent of a dowry. The most prized career is that of a civil servant. According to Greek law, it is impossible to be dismissed from this type of job, so a young woman who enters marriage with such employment, in effect, enters with a dowry of perpetual income!

A Greek home. It is common for children to stay with their parents even after marriage, usually to look after them in their old age or to manage the family business.

During the rite of baptism, water is poured over the head to symbolize acceptance into the church and the blessing of the Holy Spirit.

BABY BOOM

Children are greatly loved by Greek adults and are usually viewed as a necessary fulfillment of marriage. Again, the concept of honor is associated with producing children. Manhood depends, in part, on the ability to produce a son; a daughter is better than remaining childless. For the woman, the ideal is to become a mother and raise children who have the appropriate cultural values.

The birth of a child is a major event, especially for the first child. The rites to adulthood begin during baptism. When a name is given in the presence of the priest, godparents and parents, the child receives his or her religious, regional and national identity. A *chrismation*, or confirmation, ceremony follows the baptism. The child receives the "gift of the Spirit" after being anointed with special myrrh from the patriarchate of Constantinople. This marks the child's official membership in the Greek Orthodox Church.

In the first four years of life, Greek children are quite indulged by both parents. Father usually takes on the role of disciplinarian while mother becomes the source of love and solace. By age six, Greek children are considered responsible family members who also have the obligation of maintaining the family honor, and they become increasingly aware of *philotimo* to ensure that they will have the respect of others.

Among the many attentions given to Greek children is strong verbal interaction. Because the ability to communicate is such a valued social skill, parents like to make sure their children will be able to entertain, argue and convince by means of language. This too, they feel, is essential to bolstering or maintaining self-esteem.

DEATH RITUALS

Death rituals in Greece are marked by mourners wearing black, ritual dress during funeral wakes and memorial services.

The most important memorial services take place 40 days after death and again on the one-year anniversary. A standard aspect of the funeral process is an exhumation of the body to remove the bones for placement in an ossuary, which is a depository for the bones of the dead.

Rituals that mark transitions from one stage of life to another are considered by Greeks to be similar in nature. For example, mourning songs and wedding songs are much the same, and it is not uncommon for an unmarried woman to be buried in a wedding dress.

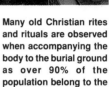
Many old Christian rites and rituals are observed when accompanying the body to the burial ground as over 90% of the population belong to the Greek Orthodox Church.

RELIGION

THE OFFICIAL RELIGION OF GREECE is Greek Orthodox. It is an autonomous faction of the Eastern Orthodox Church, an ancient form of Christianity. Today, Greece remains the only country that is officially Orthodox. While there is tolerance for other beliefs in Greece, the constitution refers to the Orthodox Church as the established religion, and proselytizing by other religious groups is forbidden. More than 95% of all Greeks are members of the Greek Orthodox Church; the remaining 5% are Moslems, Protestants, Jews and Roman Catholics.

Christianity was brought to Greece at the beginning of the 1st century by St. Paul. But it wasn't until A.D. 313 when Emperor Constantine was converted after seeing a vision of a cross in the sky, that Christianity became the official religion of the Roman Empire.

Constantine was also responsible for setting up a new capital in the East called Constantinople. This effectively split the empire into two political halves: the West speaking Latin, the East Greek. The bishop in Constantinople, the Patriarch, became second in power to the Pope in Rome who was considered the first among equals. Conflicts arose from the start. With geographic and cultural differences growing, ideological differences deepened.

The key disagreement arose when the Pope insisted that he had powers over the entire church, while the Patriarch held firm that decisions on matters of faith must be made by a council. Another difference was the question of whether priests could marry. The final division occurred in 1054 when the Patriarch of Constantinople and the Pope excommunicated one another. From that time on, the Patriarch represented the Eastern Church and the Pope headed the Roman Catholic Church.

The Orthodox Church is now the third largest branch of Christianity with about 150 million members worldwide, of whom 10 million are within Greece.

To be Greek is to be Greek Orthodox.

Opposite: **Religion is, for historical reasons, considered to be part of Greek culture. Though the Greeks do not profess to being a religious people, nonetheless, their firm belief is reflected on the altars and facades of many Greek homes.**

CHURCH AUTHORITIES

The Eastern Orthodox Church was steadfast in its belief that the old ways were best. Today, many Christian beliefs and practices remain unchanged since the first millennium. The word "orthodox," in fact, means correct belief in Greek, emphasizing that it is devoted to the original faith.

The Greek Orthodox Church has been independent of Eastern Orthodox patriarchal authority since Greece regained independence in 1833. It is now governed by the Holy Synod. This governing body is actually a convention of bishops that meets once a year under the chairmanship of the Archbishop of Athens.

There is no Orthodox figure that is comparable to the Pope. The Patriarch of Constantinople is the patriarch of all the Orthodox churches and, like the various archbishops, has the honor and esteem of fellow leaders. He is not, however, considered infallible like the Pope. This concept is consistent with the ancient Christian emphasis on the equality of all bishops.

RELIGION IN MODERN GREECE

For centuries, religion has been closely associated with Greek nationalism. During the years of Turkish rule under the Ottoman Empire, the Church served to unite all Greeks. The Patriarchate of Constantinople maintained both spiritual and civil powers over the Greek population, while monks and village priests held secret classes to preserve the Greek language and the Orthodox faith. Churches soon became sanctuaries dedicated to the preservation of culture and faith.

All over Greece, from urban centers to little villages by the sea, you will find a chapel or place of worship.

The year for many rural Greeks is based on the festivals of the church calendar. Events throughout the year, such as the harvest or the return of the fishing fleet, are marked by small religious ceremonies. The priest may be asked to give blessings at the opening of a new shop. Even birthdays do not hold as much importance as a patron saint's day.

Local churches are usually the focus of a community. All projects concerning the house of worship are a means of drawing villagers together to work for a common cause. Competitiveness and minor squabbles among families, which are familiar scenes of village life, are forgotten when the church needs to be renovated or repaired.

The Greeks consider themselves very religious; they are baptized, married and buried in church. They do not, however, necessarily attend church on a regular basis as it is not obligatory.

What is consistent among all Greeks is that the home will have a special corner for devotion containing icons (religious paintings on wood), special lamps and holy oil and water. Greeks will also light a candle to the saint most likely to solve their problem, or even buy a small token depicting what concerns them to place in front of the icon.

FROM THE PEAK OF MOUNT OLYMPUS

The gods of Greek mythology represent the attempt of a highly imaginative people to account for the world of nature and the facts of life when science was nearly unknown. Because the ancient Greeks had no explanation for the moon and the stars moving across the sky at night, or thunder in the heavens when it rained, they invented the gods and goddesses to explain these phenomena. Weaknesses and virtues of human nature were reflected in the stories or myths about the deities which date back to as early as 700 B.C. These myths were passed down from generation to generation through storytelling and poetry, and are preserved for the ages in the works of classical Greek writers. Homer's *Iliad* and *Odyssey*, and Hesiod's *Theogony* incorporate most of the characters and themes of classical Greek mythology.

The *Theogony*, in fact, describes the origin and history of the gods. According to this work, the state of emptiness in which the universe began was Chaos. From Chaos sprang Gaea or Earth, who gave birth to Uranus (Heaven). These two, as rulers of the universe, became parents of the Titans. From two of the Titans, Cronus and Rhea, came six children who were known as the gods.

The celestial gods were thought to dwell in the sky or on Mount Olympus in Thessaly. Earthbound deities were believed to live on or under the earth. Leading the ranks of the deities

APOLLO   **ATHENA**   **HERMES**

was Zeus, who was believed to be the father of the gods and men. Hera, his wife, was the queen of the heavens and the goddess of marriage. The greater gods of the heavens were Hephaestus, the god of fire; Athena, the goddess of wisdom and war; Apollo, god of light, music and poetry; Artemis, goddess of wild life and the moon; Ares, god of war; Aphrodite, goddess of love; Hermes, the gods' messenger to man and later god of science and invention; and Hestia, goddess of the hearth.

There were also lesser deities such as the nymphs, who guarded nature, and the Fates, who controlled the destiny of all humans. The nine muses were the goddesses of certain arts and sciences. All of these deities were the subject of specific myths or tales.

Because each god or goddess ruled over some part of the world or the lives of humans, ancient Greeks would idolize the particular deity that could have an effect on their problem. Poseidon, god of the waters, could oversee a successful voyage; Athena, with all her wisdom, could help a person solve a problem.

Ancient peoples throughout the world had their own gods and goddesses who were associated with supernatural powers and mythological stories. Norse, Chinese and Egyptian mythologies have characters that are quite similar to some of the Greek deities. Roman mythology is nearly identical to that of the Greeks, for when the Romans conquered the Greeks, they simply gave many of the Greek gods Roman names.

APHRODITE **ZEUS**

WEARING THE ROBES

In contrast to the Roman Catholic clergy, Orthodox priests can marry. But if a man is unmarried at the time he is ordained, then he may not marry later. And if the wife of a priest dies, he is not allowed to remarry. Married priests cannot become bishops; only those who are celibate are eligible. The head of the Greek Orthodox Church is the archbishop of Athens; he is given the title Primate of Greece.

Rural priests are often men of little schooling who receive small salaries from the government. Because married priests cannot rise to higher office, it has been customary for them to receive two years of theological training after high school rather than higher religious education.

In order to support their families, rural priests usually must work the land, just like the other villagers. Although the priest is respected for his special duties and obligations, villagers do not hold the local priests in awe. They are regarded as family men with the same pressures to provide for their families as the parishioners.

Greek Orthodox clergymen wear flowing black robes and tall black rimless hats. For the church service, colorful brocade vestments are added. Greek clergy do not shave or cut their hair, which is tied in a coiled knot at the base of their necks.

THE MONASTIC LIFE

Monasteries play an important role in the Orthodox Church. Since pre-Christian times Hellenistic peoples have been devoted to spiritual discipline and contending with the devil, passing the day in prayer and meditation. Unlike their counterparts in the Catholic Church, Orthodox monks are usually laymen.

Mount Athos, near Thessaloníki, is famous for its many monasteries,

Above: **Greek Orthodox priests are easily recognizable in their black robes and distinctive hats.**

Opposite top and bottom: **Monasteries in Greece range from beautiful and charming cloisters to inaccessible and isolated retreats.**

some of which date back to the 10th century. This religious haven has been granted independent status from Greece, and only men are allowed to visit the area. Through the 1,000-year history of Greek monastic life, the numbers of monks in monasteries have at times been high and at other periods quite low. Surprisingly, in the last 20 years there has been a resurgence in interest among young men in leading a spiritual life. About 1,500 monks currently live on this historic mountain.

There are three types of Orthodox monks. Those who live in a community and share meals, property, services and work are cenobitic monks. Idiorrhythmic monks live in small settlements and pray according to their own schedule, only coming together with other monks on feast days and Sundays. Anchorites are monks who live in remote places as hermits.

Above: **Going home after the Sunday morning service.**

Opposite: **Icons are a common sight on most altars in Greek homes.**

SUNDAY AT CHURCH

A Sunday church service can last up to three hours. In rural houses of worship or very traditional urban churches, women stay on the left side of the church, and men stay on the right. Children gather near a platform close to the front of the church. There are no pews; usually people stand or move about. The entire service is chanted.

There are no statues in Orthodox churches. Instead there are beautiful icons, which play a very important part in the Orthodox faith. Icons are traditional pictorial representations painted on wooden panels or done in mosaic or enamel. Worshipers traditionally kiss the icon of Christ first, followed by the icon of the Virgin Mary, and then the saints. Icons are thought to be a type of opening between heaven and earth through which those in heaven reveal themselves. Because of this, it is imperative that the images on the icons match all previous images of that saint. Because there is so little variation, sometimes only experts can correctly determine when older icons were painted. Creating icons is a holy task, often undertaken by several monks, each of whom specializes in a particular part, such as the hand or the face.

SUPERSTITIONS

Although Christianity replaced the pagan beliefs of the Greeks nearly 1,700 years ago, some remnants of the ancient beliefs survive today. These superstitions actually defy the teachings of the Church.

approach
do's

Witches, or occult doctors, are frequently called upon to minister to the sick. It is thought that more than 15,000 professional astrologers and fortune-tellers work in Greece at the present time. Sacrificial animal offerings still take place, as do ancient springtime rituals. For example, in the village of Gouménissa, a traditional sacrifice of a calf occurs yearly at a wayside chapel and the occasion is celebrated by folk dancing and feasting.

ANASTENARIA—FIREWALKING

Anastenaria is a ritual of firewalking and spirit possession that takes place in the Macedonian villages of Ayía Elenia and Langadhás. Kostilides, a group of refugees and their descendants from eastern Thrace who settled in the 1920s in Greek Macedonia, perform these rites. Spirit possession is thought to be a powerful vehicle by which people can come to terms with or even resolve problems by becoming one with the spirit so they acquire the power to be healed.

The cycle of events reaches a climax on May 21, which is the day the Greek Orthodox Church celebrates the festival of Saints Constantine and Helen. St. Constantine, the founder of the Byzantine Empire and savior of the Christian religion, is thought to have the power to both cause and heal a variety of illnesses. He is further believed to possess the ritual dancers and protect them from harm as they move across the hot coals. At the beginning, the dance is one of suffering, but it transforms into one of joy.

Anastenarides claim to feel warmth, but no pain. There is great satisfaction after leaving the fire, for the participants feel they have acted according to the will of the saint; if they had followed their own wills they would be punished. The rites, however, remain in conflict with the doctrine of the Orthodox Church.

LANGUAGE

GREEK, THE OFFICIAL LANGUAGE of Greece, has been spoken for nearly 4,000 years, making it the oldest oral language of Europe. And when other European societies had not yet developed written language, the Greeks were cultivating a rich literary collection.

Greek is often referred to as one of the most admirable instruments of communication ever devised. It is said to be satisfactory for both thinkers and poets. Greek remains the language of choice for a number of scholars and poets of many nationalities because they feel that no other language can so adequately convey meaning and beauty.

Greece is linguistically homogeneous, which means that almost everyone speaks the same language. For the past 30 years the census has not needed to record language data. Those who do not speak the mother tongue, about 2% of the population, speak one of the following languages: a Romanian dialect called Vlach, Turkish, Macedo-Slav and Albanian or Pomak, which is a Bulgarian dialect.

Modern Greek is a direct descendant of the Proto-Indo-European language that was spoken centuries before Christ by civilizations on the Aegean Islands, the Greek mainland and Asia Minor. Proto-Indo-European is the same language family from which many European languages are derived, but Greek does not bear any close affiliation with other languages in the family because it evolved through the centuries in relative isolation. What distinguishes Greek from other isolated languages is that many people still speak it, and early written records of ancient Greek still exist.

Ancient Greek inscribed on stone ruins.

THE ALPHABET

The Greek alphabet is composed of 24 letters that at first glance look very intimidating. It is, in fact, much simpler than the English alphabet. The pronunciation rules for the Greek alphabet are regular and, therefore, easier to master. Because alphabets ideally attempt to indicate separate sounds by separate symbols, it may be said that Greek has an ideal alphabet. And perhaps this is quite appropriate, for the word "alphabet" is based on the first two letters of the Greek alphabet!

In Greek it is quite important to correctly stress the syllables of a word. Meaning can be dependent on stress; that is, a word pronounced with the stress on the first syllable may have an entirely different meaning from the same word with the stress on the third syllable.

The alphabets of all major European languages, to some extent, are based on the ancient Greek alphabet. The Roman alphabet (the one used for this text) is sometimes called the western form of the Greek alphabet.

Letter	Name	Pronunciation	Letter	Name	Pronunciation
A	alpha	'a' as in father	N	nu	'n' as in nose
B	beta	'b' as in biology	Ξ	xi	'x' as in fix
Γ	gamma	'g' as in guild	O	omicron	'o' as in hot
Δ	delta	'd' as in democracy	Π	pi	'p' as in pie
E	epsilon	'e' as in get	P	rho	'r' as in rhinoceros
Z	zeta	'z' as in zoo	Σ	sigma	's' as in signal
H	eta	'a' as in paper	T	tau	't' as in temple
Θ	theta	'th' as in theater	Υ	upsilon	'ee' as in feet
I	iota	'i' as in police	Φ	phi	'ph' as in philodendron
K	kappa	'k' as in kitten	X	chi	'ch' as in chorus
Λ	lambda	'l' as in lion	Ψ	psi	'ps' as in eclipse
M	mu	'm' as in miss	Ω	omega	'o' as in oral

DIALECTS

A unique aspect of today's Greek language is that it is really composed of two dialects: *dimotiki* and *katharévousa*. *Dimotiki*, or demotic Greek, is rooted in ancient Greek. Historically, demotic Greek was the language of the common people. It continues to be used today in casual speech by all Greeks.

Katharévousa means "pure." When Greece regained its independence in the 1830s, scholars created a superior language based on the classical tongue. This artificial language became the official state language in 1836. Everything was written in *katharévousa*, from laws and documents to magazines and nursery rhymes.

Much opposition to this pure language evolved for a number of reasons. Educated people objected to writing in what was actually a dead language. Teachers and schoolchildren found it difficult because it is very challenging to teach or learn a language that is never spoken. Also, people from small villages who did not have the advantage of formal education were effectively prevented from becoming literate. Their inability to learn it kept the villagers among the lower classes.

Opposition to *katharévousa* became so prominent that demotic Greek was declared the official language in 1975. After the law was passed, the

There are over 100 daily newspapers in Greece. Censorship laws extend only to articles offensive to religious sensitivities or scandalous to the president.

most immediate change was that *katharévousa* was dropped from the curriculum at all educational levels. *Katharévousa*, however, remains a part of the written language because government publications, religious documents and books written before the mid-1970s exist in the old form.

Dialects were more numerous in ancient times: Mycenaean, Aeolic, Doric and Attic-Ionic to name a few. Attic was the dialect of Athens, and because Athens was the center of prestige in ancient times, the Attic dialect became the standard for the entire Greek-speaking world. This dialect superseded the other Hellenic dialects, and demotic Greek spoken today is a natural development of the Attic dialect.

GREEK INFLUENCE ON THE ENGLISH LANGUAGE

Loan words are a tremendous contribution to all languages, and English is one of the greatest beneficiaries of such borrowings. Latin and Greek are quite prevalent in our language. Some Greek words in our vocabulary are acronym, agnostic, autocracy, chlorine, kudos, pathos, telegram and xylophone.

Sometimes, the borrowed element is a root which serves as the basis for longer words. English has many such Greek roots. On the right are some Greek roots that, in combination with other words, form the English language we use every day.

Root	Meaning	English words
autos	self	autograph, automatic
biblios	book	biblical, bibliography
cryptos	secret	crypt, cryptic
dynamis	power	dynamic, dynamite
graphein	writing	graphic, graphite
homos	same	homogenize, homonym
logy	study of	geology, biology
micro	small	microcosm, microbe
neos	new	neon, neolithic
orthos	right	orthodontic, orthopedic
philos	love	philanthropy, philosophy
scope	watch	telescope, microscope
tele	far	television, telephone

GESTURES

Gestures are a very important channel of communication. However, people tend to assume that they have universal meaning. This, of course, is far from true. One different but delightful gesture any American visitor to a Greek home will experience is to be greeted with a hug and a kiss on both cheeks.

Greeks are eager to argue about anything, but it is more of a lively pastime than a disagreement. An important part of this activity is the almost frantic arm-waving that accompanies the dramatic wordplay. Almost as proof that the arguments are not serious, Greeks generally calm down quite quickly after a heated conversation.

While Greeks do not have an entirely different set of gestures from Americans, there are some distinctions that are worth noting.

1. Crossed fingers, which usually signify hope or wishing for Americans, is the sign of two people with some kind of close relationship, romantic.

2. A pursed hand gesture is a sign of excellence.

3. Pulling on the lower eyelid is an indication of superiority or disbelief.

4. The head tossed jerkily upwards in a backward motion is the equivalent of a side-to-side head shake to indicate "no."

5. Greeks do not wave in the same manner as Americans; in fact it is an insult to show the palm with the fingers extended. Greeks wave with the index finger raised and the palm closed.

6. Greeks will make a puff of breath through pursed lips after receiving a compliment. This is a superstition meant to protect them from the "evil eye."

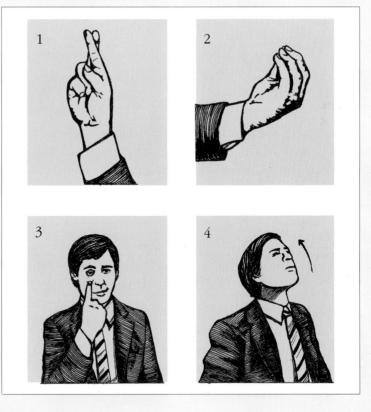

ARTS

WHEN PERICLES SET OUT TO RESTORE Athens after the Battle of Salamis, he not only supervised a very successful rebuilding program, but he attracted the best Greek artists and scholars to the city. During the remarkable era known as the Golden Age, the arts flourished.

The ancient Greeks were among the earliest to separate religion from the study of ideas and knowledge—a discipline that became known as philosophy. The philosophical writings of the Golden Age are still read today, as are other literary works. Poetry and drama developed during the Golden Age with epic and lyric poetry and comic and tragic dramas emerging as the most enduring forms.

The Greeks were also quite active in architecture, sculpture and painting. They created architectural styles that set standards for the future. In sculpture, the Greeks produced what is considered to be the ideal form. And though no original Greek paintings have survived, much is known of their beauty because there are vivid descriptions of them found in ancient Greek writings.

Western civilization is based on the contribution of the Greeks, many of which are in the field of the arts and letters.

LITERATURE IN ANCIENT GREECE

Greek literature, which dates back to the second millennium B.C., is the most influential national literature in the Western world. It was the model for all literature in the West, from Latin literature onward. Tragic and comic drama, lyric and epic poetry, philosophical essays and dialogues, literary letters, critical and biographical history are types of literature that were introduced by Greek writers.

EARLY GREEK LITERATURE The first significant Greek literary form was epic poetry—narrative poems that tell about heroic deeds of gods and men. Homer, perhaps the greatest Greek poet, composed the *Iliad* and the *Odyssey* around 700 B.C. These poems, which emphasized the ideals of honor and bravery, greatly influenced Greek culture and education.

An early Greek vase portrays a scene from Homer's *Odyssey*. The hero, Odysseus, is tied to the mast of his ship to protect himself from the song of the sirens which drives men to destroy their ships.

Another important epic poem was *Theogony*, by Hesiod. Written around 600 B.C., *Theogony* organized the origin and history of the Greek gods. Another monumental work of Hesiod was *Works and Days*, which described the life of the Greek peasant farmers.

Lyric poetry emerged around 650 B.C. Lyrics were much shorter than epics, and they generally described personal feelings rather than acts of valor. Lyric poetry was also sung to the music of the lyre. Another form of lyric poetry is the choral lyric, sung by groups and accompanied by music and dancing. Sappho and Pindar are the best known lyric poets.

THE GOLDEN AGE The 30-year period (461–431 B.C.) in which the arts, especially literature, flourished is known as the Golden Age. Drama emerged as an important literary form. Aeschylus, Euripides and Sophocles were the three great tragic playwrights of the Golden Age. Comedic drama was just as popular and none were more famous than the works of Aristophanes. They reflected the spirited sense of freedom and vitality felt by the Athenians and their ability to laugh at themselves. The masterful use of the language and complexity of thought and insight are works of genius that are still enjoyed today.

Prose replaced poetry as the leading literary form by the end of the 400s B.C., and historical writings became quite popular. Herodotus, called the "Father of History," recorded the cultural characteristics of the civilized world, focusing on the conflict of East and West.

Another great literary form arising during the Golden Age was rhetoric, which is the art of persuasive writing and speech. An invention of the sophists, or teacher-philosophers, rhetoric was a major factor for the rise in popularity of prose over poetry.

Socrates, who died in 399 B.C., left no written works, but he is indirectly responsible for another influential literary invention—philosophical dialogue. The Socratic method of examining ideas was the basis of philosophical dialogue, and through Socrates's students (especially Plato) the ideas of Socrates live on. Plato's ideas were also recorded for the ages by his students, the most well-known of whom was Aristotle.

Busts of Sophocles, Aristophanes and Euripides.

A work of Byzantine art created in the 6th century. By then, Greece had been exposed to and influenced by the many different artforms of the East and West.

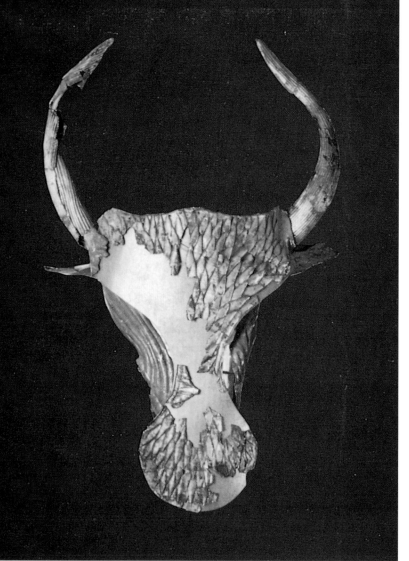

THE HELLENISTIC AND BYZANTINE PERIODS After the death of Alexander the Great came the establishment of the Roman Empire. Alexandria replaced Athens as the capital of Greek civilization. A new literary style, pastoral poetry, developed around 200 B.C. It described the loveliness of nature and country life.

Prose also continued to develop. Plutarch, considered a historian, was actually a biographer whose works have provided much information for historians. *Parallel Lives*, his most famous work, shows his desire for Greek culture to be encouraged and preserved in the Roman world.

When Constantinople became the center of Greek culture, Christian religious poetry dominated literary form. The political climate of the Byzantine Empire restricted a writer's artistic freedom but many theological and historical writings were produced at that time.

The last original literary vehicle of the ancient Greeks was the novel, dating from the 2nd and 3rd

centuries A.D. Greek novels were usually romances with complicated plots involving a hero and heroine. The most famous Greek romantic novel is *Daphnis and Chloë* written in the 3rd century A.D.

ART AND ARCHITECTURE IN ANCIENT GREECE

Art in ancient Greece was closely connected with religion. Much of art centered on the human form as the Greeks considered the gods to be in the form of perfect men and women.

Architecture, large sculpture and painting were mainly functional until the 4th century B.C. They commemorated athletic victories and religious matters. Decorative arts from this time were mainly to be found in tombs though small ceramic sculptures and statuettes could be found in the homes of private individuals. Most of the tools used by ancient Greek artists were hand tools, with the exception of the potter's wheel, which was run by a foot treadle.

The Temple of Aphaia was probably built during the Archaic period and has the Doric columns that characterize the early buildings of Greece.

91

Doric column. Examples of Doric temples still exist in Syracuse, Akragas and Metapontum, the most famous being the Parthenon in Athens.

Ionic column. These columns were developed at a later period and can be distinguished by its more ornate design. Ionic-style temples can be seen in Athens, Naucratis and Ephesus.

Right: **The changing styles of Greek art, from the abstract painting of the Geometric period to the stiff but more lifelike figure of the late Archaic period.**

THE GEOMETRIC PERIOD There were four main periods in the development of ancient Greek art and architecture. The first is known as the Geometric period (about 1100 to 700 B.C.) It is characterized by the extensive use of geometric figures and abstractions. Small pieces of bronze and clay geometric sculpture have been found, one of which is a small statuette of Apollo. It, like other pieces of this period, is a conception rather than a direct visual representation. Geometric architecture of this period is located in Sparta, Olympia and Crete. However, only the foundations of these temples remain.

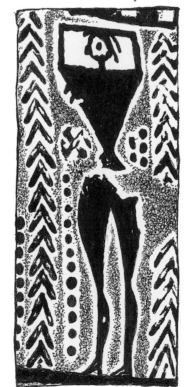

THE ARCHAIC PERIOD The Archaic period lasted from about 660 B.C. to 475 B.C. During the early Archaic period, temples of marble were built on the Aegean Islands, and limestone temples covered with marble on the mainland. Stone monuments were also created for temples. At this time, human figures had an expression known as the archaic smile, and it is thought that this was done to highlight an expression that is specific to humans only. Other significant artifacts from the early part of this period include vases painted with black figures and Corinthian-style vases which were often crowded with floral ornaments and fabulous monsters, like the Chimera.

The middle part of this period saw art drawing its inspiration from nature. Human forms became more lifelike. Paintings began to reflect three dimensions. Temples built during the middle Archaic period had six front columns and evenly spaced columns all around the outside.

Sculpture of the middle Archaic period depicted people in action, often in scenes of battle or athletic victory. Beautifully proportioned vases with jet-black glaze and lively scenes were also prevalent.

In the late Archaic period, a significant evolution occurred in vase painting. The red-figure style emerged in which figures were preserved in the red of the clay surrounded by a black background.

The Treasury of the Athenians. It was a largely Athenian navy that defeated the Persians at Salamis. After the war, many city-states joined the Delian League with the promise of protection by Athens' navy. They made regular contributions to the treasury at Athens which were used to build the temples and buildings seen today.

THE CLASSICAL PERIOD The Classical period went on from 475 B.C. to 323 B.C. In the early part of this period, Greece rebuilt many of the temples damaged during the Persian Wars. Doric-style temples were the common style. An outstanding example of this architecture is the Temple of Zeus in Olympia. Sculpture no longer had the archaic smile; it showed expressions of both seriousness and joy and more simplicity of detail. Scenes portrayed the moment before or after a significant event. Original pieces of this period are lost, but because they were greatly admired, many Roman artists made copies which still exist.

The middle Classical period saw the restoration of the many temples burned by the Persians, and work on rebuilding the Acropolis in Athens began. A monumental gateway to the Acropolis was created and the Parthenon was born. These examples are Greek Classical art at its finest!

Other significant Doric works of the period are the Hephaesteion, which still stands in Athens, the Temple of Poseidon and the Temple of Themis. Great Ionic works include the Temple of Nike, the Erechtheum and the Temple of Athena.

The outstanding sculptors of the middle Classical period were Phidias, considered the sculptor of gods, and Polyclitus, the sculptor of men. Vase painting of the middle Classical period has a linear perspective that gives figures a three-dimensional appearance.

During the late Classical period, Athens lost its political supremacy, and its architecture declined. Greek sculptures of that time, though, are considered supreme examples of Classical art. Greek paintings from the 4th century B.C. no longer exist, but the first-century A.D. paintings in Pompeii and Herculaneum were probably influenced by them. Unfired terracotta statuettes recovered mostly from tombs have survived to this day. They depict comic actors, fashionable women, dwarfs and demi-gods.

The famous sculpture of Venus de Milo is actually a representation of the Greek Goddess of Love, Aphrodite. The Romans were great admirers of Hellenistic culture, and had made many other copies of this sculpture.

THE HELLENISTIC PERIOD After the conquests of Alexander the Great, Oriental elements influenced art and architecture. Small temples continued to be built in the Doric style, although columns were usually in the Corinthian style. Gymnasiums, theaters and senate houses were among the new types of buildings that were constructed, and great ornamentation marked these edifices. Private homes changed from a rectangular hall to a rectangle built around a courtyard with columns. The arch and the vault were elements introduced to Hellenistic buildings from the Orient.

Sculpture of the Hellenistic period changed from simple, closed forms that kept the eye of the viewer on the figure to open forms that carry the eye of the viewer beyond the space occupied by the figure.

MODERN ARTS

LITERATURE For nearly 400 years during the Turkish occupation, Greek literature stagnated. Only in areas like the Ionian Islands, which never came under Ottoman rule, and Crete, Cyprus and Rhodes, which were independent at times, did literature continue to be produced.

After attaining independence in the early 1820s, Greek scholars were divided about whether to use the normal spoken form of Greek (*dimotiki* or demotic Greek) or the classical form (*katharévousa*). Many scholars thought the demotic form was vulgar and limited in its uses for literature.

But the demotic form of writing continued to gain widespread support in the 20th century and, following World War II, Greek literature became known throughout the world due to the works of poets and writers such as Constantine Cavafy, George Seferis (Nobel Prize 1963), Nikos Kazantzakis and Odysseus Elytis (Nobel Prize 1979).

Perhaps the Greek writer of greatest international renown is Nikos Kazantzakis, author of *Zorba the Greek* and *The Last Temptation of Christ*. The latter stirred up controversy when it was made into a movie. Riots broke out as many viewers considered the film to be a blasphemous interpretation of the life of Christ.

A modern representation of the Trojan Horse. According to the poem, *Iliad*, Greek soldiers hid in the horse and, when it was brought into Troy, the soldiers came out of the horse to unlock the city gates. The invading Greek soldiers then destroyed Troy.

Opposite top and bottom: The top relief comes from the Hellenistic period while the lower relief is a typical example of Classical Greek style. The ornate fashion of the former shows evidence of Oriental influence.

Concerts and plays are regularly held in these ancient ruins. These performances are very popular as they make audiences feel transported back to the times of ancient Greece.

MUSIC Music is most representative of the blending of Eastern and Western influences in Greece. When the Greeks gained their independence in 1821, they had their native folk music as well as religious music that was Byzantine in origin. When Greece became free, many Greeks living in other parts of Europe returned home bringing their European musical culture along.

Greece's new leaders introduced music instruction in the schools, imported musical instruments, organized orchestras and musical societies and were successful in reviving musical interest in the cities.

Greek music evolved through stages, from Italian-inspired music to attempts at creating a national music based on folk sounds and culminating in avant-garde music after World War II. Church music, however, remained unchanged as did the folk music of rural Greeks.

Today, Nicos Skalkotas is regarded as the originator of Greece's modern serious music. *Four Greek Dances*, a score for orchestra, is his best known composition. More recent entrants into the international music arena are composers Vangelis and singer Nana Mouskouri.

ART ·Folk art was almost the only Greek art from the classical age until Greek independence., Pottery was developed on the islands and on the southern mainland for both decorative purposes and everyday use. Simple, graceful forms were realized with what appeared to be great dexterity. Copper, bronze, iron and other metals replaced pottery in northern Greece and in other areas throughout the country.

Silver and gold jewelry were developed not only for women to wear, but for the decoration of firearms, weapons and knives. Folk costumes varied greatly with the occasion and area, but they all seemed to preserve old patterns in design, fabric and ornamentation. The types of folk art that were of exceptionally high quality were fabric weaving, embroidery and leatherwork.

The Ionian Islands developed a fine school of painting because of their freedom from Turkish occupation and the influence of the great masters of Venice. The Ionian paintings had free design in a wide range of colors.

After the liberation of Greece, many aspiring artists studied in Munich, the greatest of whom was Giannoules Halepas, whose works are the masterpieces of modern Greek sculpture.

Twentieth century Greek artists of note are landscape painters Odysseus Phocas, George Hadzopoulos and Nikolaos Othonaios, and portrait painter Spyros Vikatos.

The art of weaving and embroidery is alive in Greece. Ethnic carpets, wall-hangings and rugs can be bought in the many street-stalls of Greece.

LEISURE

THE GREEKS ARE GOOD AT LEISURE. They have such an exuberance for living that they seldom miss an opportunity to enjoy themselves. It is often difficult for them to differentiate work from leisure, for they are such spirited people that they are able to enjoy themselves any time.

Much of a Greek's leisure time is spent out of the house, due mostly to his or her aversion to solitude and love of conversation and crowds. Social life is enjoyed out in the streets and many return home only to sleep. Great fun for the Greeks is traveling around the city or town with their favorite group of friends. It is like a moving party, picking up old friends along the way or meeting new ones as they go along.

Greeks have a word for the feeling of well-being that they experience when they are sitting among friends, enjoying food, wine or coffee and having a good time. The feeling is known as *kéfi*. It is often while feeling *kéfi* that a Greek person just gets up and dances.

FOLK MUSIC

Greece's musical tradition is in its folk songs. It is one of the few artforms that continued developing during the Turkish occupation. Songs of various regions evolved from matters which affected the people. For example, *klephtic* ("KLEF-tik") ballads were songs from the mountains that told of battles, heroic deeds and painful defeats. On the other hand, music from the islands was smooth and disarming. The songs of the valleys and plains told of enslaved persons and their struggle for independence.

Greek folk songs mark every occasion. There are distinct forms for weddings, feasts, the welcoming of the seasons, lullabies and funerals. Mourning songs are emphasized by wailing and moaning. Byzantine chants, often the only other type of music heard by the Greeks during the centuries of Turkish rule, had much influence on folk music.

Opposite: **The modern-day Olympic Stadium in Athens, Greece. The Olympic Games originated here in Olympia around 776 B.C. as a religious festival held in honor of Zeus, god of the sky. The first games of the modern Olympics were held in Athens in 1896.**

Below: **The banjo-like instrument is called the** *bouzoúki.* **It is used to accompany nostalgic Greek folk songs known as** *rembétika.*

FOLK DANCING

Dancing has been a vital part of Greek life since the beginning of time. Archeologists have found evidence that as early as 1400 B.C., dancing played an important part in religious ceremonies. A Cretan sword dance performed today was described in the *Iliad*. As before, each Greek ceremony continues to have its own dances, whether solemn or festive.

Dancing is to the Greeks not only an artistic form of self expression; it is often a release for bottled-up emotions and is done at times that Americans might consider inappropriate. It is not unusual for a Greek person, upon hearing dreadful news, to stand up and start dancing alone.

Greek dances are usually performed by a group of people, arm-in-arm in a line or open circle moving counter-clockwise. The leader of the group often improvises while the followers usually adhere to a basic step. The hundreds of Greek dances have different names, and they are often variations of one another. The *tavérna* is one place to see some creative, invigorating dance.

THE FOLK DANCES OF GREECE

Zeibekiko is commonly seen in *tavérnas*, danced alone or face-to-face with another person. Sometimes called the "dance of the eagle," participants hold out their arms like wings and slowly circle each other in a dance of combat. When done by a single dancer, he or she performs around an imaginary opponent. Often, the dancer seems to be in a trance, with eyes staring down. Spectators respect the privacy of the performer by never applauding or commenting on the act, for it is executed solely for the experience of the dancer alone.

Another popular dance is the *hasapiko*, or butcher's dance. Two or three men dance this slow, sad dance. With arms on each other's shoulders they dance the same basic steps in a solemn, tense style that is meant to help release emotions.

The *tsamiko* is a line dance that is sometimes called the "handkerchief dance" because the leader and person next to him hold on to a handkerchief. The leader, however, is expected to perform acrobatic stunts with the handkerchief providing support while held by the second dancer! This dance was performed widely by freedom fighters in the war for independence.

The *kalamatiano* is considered by many to be the national dance of Greece. It is a happy, light dance, the name of which is derived from its place of origin. It, too, is a line dance where participants hold hands at shoulder height.

Ski enthusiasts head for the mountains of central Greece where there are several ski centers.

SPORTS

Soccer, or *podosphéro* ("pod-AHS-fay-roh"), as it is called in Greek, is the national pastime. Soccer is one of the favorite topics of discussion, after politics. It is said that the only time the streets are empty in Greek cities is when the Greek national soccer team match is televised, usually on Wednesdays. Greece also has a soccer league of 16 teams that play against one another on Sundays. Greeks are as devoted to this professional league as Americans are to major league baseball or professional football.

Another sport that is gaining in popularity is basketball. In 1987, Greece made its mark on the international sports scene by capturing the world basketball title. As a result, basketball teams are popping up all over the country and the sport is enthusiastically practiced on the courts by students of all ages.

Water sports, including yacht racing, are of great interest to the Greeks. Children learn to swim at a very early age because the clear Greek waters are so inviting. Sailing, diving and rowing regattas also draw many enthusiasts. Thousands of spectators will also crowd the stands every year for the Acropolis Rally. So it is no surprise that automobile racing has gained much popularity in Greece over the last few decades.

THE OLYMPICS

The Greeks held Zeus, king of the gods, in great honor, and they built many temples for him, one of which was in southwestern Greece, at Olympia. To pay even greater tribute to him, they established the Olympic Games around 776 B.C.

The games took place in a meadow near the Alpheus River. Not only did the best athletes compete, but the finest artisans contested for distinction in their respective fields. The ideal man to the Greeks was one who could perform amazing physical feats as well as write poetry, so it is not surprising that the first Olympics were all-around competitions.

The first recorded winner of a sports event was a cook named Coroebus, who finished first in a foot race. According to legend, the race was 200 yards long, which was the distance Hercules could walk while holding his breath.

The Olympic Games became an important forum for the exchange of ideas among the leading men of Greece. The games became so much a part of the national life that four-year periods were referred to as "olympiads" by the 4th century B.C. Peace reigned when the Olympic Games were held; all wars and quarrels were put aside.

As the number of events expanded, various structures were built to accommodate them: a hippodrome for chariot races, a gymnasium and baths. Events focused on the skills that were essential to survival in Greece at that time. Men were expected to keep in top physical shape to be ready to defend their city-states. The only prizes awarded were olive wreaths from sacred groves.

The amateur status of Olympic athletes has been an important aspect of the games since ancient times. But extreme competitiveness caused bribery and violations of the Olympic code of honor. This eventually led Roman emperor Theodosius I to ban the games in A.D. 393 after nearly 1,200 years of recorded Olympic history.

In 1896, Baron Pierre de Coubertin revived the Olympic Games in Athens as a means of building friendship among the countries of the world. Athletes from all over the world competed in the spirit of ancient Greek ideals. By the third modern Olympic Games, women athletes were permitted to compete in archery and, by 1928, they were vying for honors in swimming, and track and field.

Tom Selleck will be speaking Greek in this dubbed version of Magnum P.I. Even old American programs are very popular on Greek television.

MOVIES AND TELEVISION

Perhaps one of the reasons so much activity takes place out on the streets is because the Greeks are dissatisfied with the quality of their movies and television programs. As these industries are regulated by the government, people complain that plots are uninspiring, programs are not changed frequently enough and the news presented is often very one-sided or incomplete.

In recent years, going to the movies has grown in popularity. Many new movie theaters have been built in middle-class neighborhoods. They screen foreign films from the United States, Britain, France and Germany. Greek films are made on a limited budget and consequently, standards are not very high. These movies appeal mostly to provincial audiences.

THEATER

The summer season is a particularly exciting time for theater in Greece, for it takes place in open-air theaters from June through September.

One such event, the Athens Festival, has a varied program of concerts, dances and ancient drama. Popular with Greeks and tourists alike, performances are held in the ancient theater of Herodotus of Attica on the steps of the Acropolis. Another famous celebration of theater is the Epidaurus Festival, devoted only to the production of ancient tragedies and comedies. This 14,000-seat arena dates back to the 3rd century B.C.

The magnificent theaters of Greece would later influence many Roman amphitheaters which can still be found in France and all the way to Turkey.

FESTIVALS

IN GREECE, A DAY HARDLY PASSES WITHOUT A CELEBRATION of some kind. In fact, until quite recently, Greek civil servants had 25 religious holidays during the year!

Since the Eastern Orthodox Church adopted the Gregorian calendar instead of the Julian calendar in the 1920s, most religious holidays in Greece fall at the same time of the year as they do for the rest of the world. The exceptions to this are the holidays of Easter and Whitsun (a feast on the seventh Sunday after Easter), which are still based on the Julian calendar.

Opposite: **Festivals in Greece are a celebration of color and life as people dress in folk costumes to celebrate into the night.**

CALENDAR OF EVENTS

Jan	Feast of St. Basil the Great
	Twelfth Night
	Feast of the Epiphany
	Hellenic Letters Day,
	Festival of Schools
Mar	Independence Day
	The Annunciation of the Virgin
	Easter
Apr	Feast of St. George,
	Patron of Shepherds
May	Labor Day and Flower Festival
Aug	Dormition of the Virgin Mary
	Festival of the Countryside
Oct	St. Demetrios' Day,
	Festival of Demetria
	Ochi Day

Dec	St. Nicholas' Day
	Feast of St. Spyridon
	Christmas

FESTIVALS OF LOCAL PATRON SAINTS

Every village celebrates its own festival on the day of its patron saint. This is the saint to whom the local church is dedicated, or the saint that holds a special vocation for the villagers. For example, the principal religious festival on Corfu, which is an island port, is dedicated to St. Spyridon. He is the patron saint of seamen.

All small village communities organize their own merrymaking for the festival of the chapel's saint. It begins with the celebration of the Mass with many twinkling candles lighting up the church. After Mass, the congregation shares in a huge meal cooked by the church council and then the singing and dancing goes on until dusk. Church bells peal the whole day through to inform other villages of the festival.

Religious ceremonies are not always solemn and somber affairs. After Mass, people celebrate with dancing, singing and feasting.

CHRISTMAS

On Christmas eve, especially in villages, children go from house to house singing carols. The celebration of Christmas in Greece does not have the gift-giving or merriment that it does in Western countries. Families do, however, have a festive Christmas dinner, which is the culmination of a 25-day "little Lent" period.

A wooden cross wrapped with a sprig of basil is the symbol for Christmas in Greece, for the basil is thought to ward off the *kallikantzare* ("kahl-eek-ahnt-ZAh-reh") which are mischievous creatures that will disturb the household during the 12 days from Christmas to Epiphany. They would knock over chairs, put out fires and cause other minor accidents in the house. The woman of the home sprinkles basil-soaked water throughout the house to ward off these spirits.

ST. BASIL'S DAY

St. Basil's Day, which falls on New Year's Day, is a time for parties, presents and good luck charms. St. Basil is the patron saint of the poor and needy. Gift-giving takes place in Greece on St. Basil's Day, and a special dessert, St. Basil's cake, is served. A small coin is baked in the pastry to symbolize St. Basil's generosity. The person who finds it is thought to have good luck for the coming year.

Rural Greeks traditionally go visiting on this day and they customarily take some sand or a stone to the home they are visiting. The presentation of the sand or stone is said to ensure a good crop in the coming year. The stones and sand are kept in a pile for eight days before being discarded.

Party dress for the Greek women on the island of Corfu.

EPIPHANY

Epiphany is the culmination of the Christmas season. In the Greek Orthodox Church, the "Blessing of the Waters" takes place on Epiphany eve (Twelfth Night) and Epiphany. On Epiphany eve, priests go from house to house to sprinkle holy water. In some communities, a procession of carolers follows the priest.

The most important "Blessing of the Waters" ceremony takes place on Epiphany, January 6. The event is of great importance to Greek seamen whose vessels have been idle for the 12 days from Christmas to Epiphany. All vessels large and small are decorated and a church procession makes its way to the harbor carrying a cross that is ceremonially thrown into the sea. This is the signal for church bells to ring, ships' horns to blow and warships to fire their cannons. Young men dive into the water to retrieve the cross, and the fellow who emerges with it is presented with gifts and the honor of carrying the cross throughout the village for the day.

NAME DAY

In Greece, people celebrate their name day rather than their birthday. The name day will be the feast day of their patron saint. For example, on June 29 during the feast of Saints Peter and Paul, all men and boys named Peter or Paul will celebrate. Men and women usually stay home from work on their name days, and parties are usually thrown for children and their friends. It is also customary for adults to welcome friends to their home on name days. A special church service is held for all the people celebrating their name day, and those honored take token gifts to their friends in addition to receiving gifts on that day.

INDEPENDENCE DAY AND OCHI DAY

In this very religious country, there are two political holidays that are also held sacred. They are Independence Day and Ochi Day.

The War of Independence against Turkey began on March 25, 1821 as an armed uprising. After nearly four centuries of Turkish rule, the Greeks won their freedom in July of 1822. Every year on March 25th, the Greeks celebrate their independence with fireworks.

October 28 is Ochi Day. *Ochi* ("OH-kee") is the Greek word for "no." The origin of this festival can be traced back to 1940 when the Greek prime minister told Benito Mussolini that Italian troops could not enter the country to build military bases on Greek soil. War broke out between Italy and Greece and, much to the world's surprise, the poorly armed Greeks defeated the Italian army. Though the Germans eventually overran Greece, beginning the long German occupation, the Greeks commemorate the successful resistance to Italian troops.

A church procession on Easter Sunday.

EASTER SEASON

Easter is by far the most important holiday in the Greek Orthodox Church. It is celebrated according to the Julian calendar, usually falling one week later than it does in Western churches. Easter is deeply rooted in the Greek heart and soul; most Greeks return to their home village just for the celebrations. The Greek word for Easter is *Lambri,* which means "Bright Day."

Easter season begins with Carnival about three weeks before Lent. On the last night of the celebrations, people eat and revel throughout the night for the last time before the fasting for Lent begins.

"Clean Monday" signifies the beginning of Lent and is a day of fasting. On this day, Greeks will eat only unleavened bread and, traditionally, will climb a mountain to fly a kite, a symbol of release. During Lent, many Greeks do not eat meat or olive oil and they do not drink wine.

On Good Friday, total fasting is observed. Funeral services to mark the death of Christ are held in all churches. The next day, Holy Saturday, a Resurrection Mass is celebrated and, at midnight, the clergy and choir leave the church to chant hymns in the streets. Worshipers light candles

Ever since Byzantine times, Greek festivals have revolved around the Christian calendar. Churches themselves support and encourage the local arts by promoting traditional dances.

and the priest exclaims, "*Christos anesti*" (Christ is risen). Parishioners respond with, "*Alithos anesti*" (Indeed, He has risen).

Everyone rushes home, pausing only to blow out the candles at the doorstep. They feast on soup and cakes. Eggs are dyed red to symbolize Christ's blood and everybody grabs one to clink it with the eggs of those around them. The egg that outlasts the rest brings luck to its holder. Fireworks explode in the sky and the feasting goes on into the night.

On Easter Sunday, the Greeks attend sunrise services in their holiday finery, dance folk dances, feast on the traditional lamb roasted on a spit and welcome the start of spring.

FOOD

EATING AND DRINKING IN GREECE are not just a means of satisfying one's hunger and thirst; meals are social events. Food and drink provide a very pleasant occasion for talking, arguing, socializing, gossiping and making deals. And Greeks seldom eat alone.

The Greeks have a culinary tradition that stretches back 2,800 years. One of the world's first cookbooks was written by Hesiod, who lived in the 8th century B.C. Literature shows that the ancient Greeks enjoyed baked fish, roast lamb, honey cakes, and used many of the herbs and spices the modern Greeks put into their pots today. It is probable that the many Greek meals eaten tonight would have been familiar to Homer, Euripides and Aristophanes!

Above: **A typical meal consists of fish, salad, bread, fruit and wine.**

Opposite: **Skewered pieces of meat and vegetable make a delicious lamb kebab.**

TRADITIONAL FOOD AND DRINK

Geography and climate have been principal influences on the cuisine of Greece. Though the Hellenic Republic is situated in Europe, it is quite close to the Middle East and many facets of Greek cookery reflect Middle Eastern influences. From history, Greece has also inherited some delectable legacies. For example, the Turks brought coffee and the Persians introduced rice, yogurt and many sweet desserts.

On the mountains roam herds of sheep and goats, and these animals provide the country's most popular meat and dairy products. Though chicken and pork are eaten here, lamb is the favorite meat, and milk from goats is used as a beverage as well as to make feta cheese.

As Greece is surrounded by the sea, fish and seafood seasoned with juicy local lemons and tangy oregano are very popular dishes.

As the visitor weaves through the crowded marketplace, he or she can also find stalls and shops that sell dried legumes like nuts, coconut, chick peas and salted seeds. A few feet away cooking utensils are for sale; next to that is the spice shop. Fortunately there is a kiosk nearby, which sells everything, for a net shopping bag is probably a wise purchase!

THE OPEN-AIR MARKET OF ATHENS

In the center of Athens on Athena Street is a market that has been thriving for decades and, though much larger, is representative of markets located in towns throughout Greece.

The fish market has always been mentioned in Greek literature; it opens early and always seems filled with shoppers. The floor is laden

with sawdust to soak up the melting ice. The air is filled with the smell of fish, and the fishmongers noisily sing praises of their goods.

The meat market nearby has whole lambs, pigs, calves, game and poultry hanging row after row on hooks. The meat vendor calls out the advantages of his fine meats and persuades passers-by to try his delicacies.

Next might be the cheese shop, where fragrant cheeses stand in huge piles while the cheese seller cuts off chunks of cheese to weigh for his customers and for handing out as sample tidbits to tempt passers-by. There are feta, *mizithra*, *kasseri*, *kefalotyri*, *graviera* and *manouri*. The cheeses range from unsalted and soft to hard, salty and strong tasting.

The beauty of the fruits and other produce might draw you into the vegetable seller's stall. The deep purple eggplant looks perfectly ripe as it sits next to the ruby-red tomatoes and beautiful green peppers. Okra and assorted greens are piled high. The warmth of the day makes the scent of the vegetables a sweet delight.

118

COOKING IN VILLAGES

Kitchens in rural homes of poor families are quite primitive. It is often no more than a tiny cupboard and an iron pot hanging over the fireplace. Water is brought in from a well because there is no indoor plumbing. There is also no refrigeration, so perishable food is stored in a screened box and hung inside the well. Baking is done in an outside oven, which is a large mound of mud shaped like a beehive, heated by burning brushwood until it is nearly red hot. The charcoal is then raked out and the food to be baked is put in. Housewives in larger villages often send the food to be baked to a large community oven tended by a baker. He watches over the baking process only. All other preparations must be done in the home.

Meals in homes with such limited facilities are usually simple. Foods are combined in a single pot and made into soup or stew. Bread and olives are the staple diet. The typical diet in poor villages consists of bread, potatoes, rice, vegetables and fruit. Lamb and chicken are eaten only on special days.

From the hooks of his stall, a butcher displays carcasses of lamb and a whole pig. In small villages, food sellers usually go from door to door. Some days a village wife will be paid a call from the fisherman with his catch, the baker, the vegetable seller and the roll vendor.

AVGOLEMONO SOUP (EGG AND LEMON SOUP)

2 quarts strong, strained chicken broth   4 eggs
½ cup uncooked rice   Juice of 2 lemons

1. Bring broth to boil and add rice. Cook until rice is tender, about 20 minutes.
2. Remove broth from heat. Just before serving, beat the eggs with a rotary beater until they are light and frothy. Slowly beat in lemon juice and dilute mixture with two cups of the hot soup, beating constantly until well mixed.
3. Add diluted egg-lemon mixture to rest of the soup, beating constantly. Bring almost to the boiling point, but do not boil or the soup will curdle.

Serve immediately.

MEALTIMES

Breakfast, lunch and dinner are the
traditional meals in Greece. Breakfast,
or *proeeno,* is a light meal, usually eaten
as early as 7 a.m. Many people have
only Greek coffee, which is a strong,
thick mixture of fine ground coffee,
sugar and water. If anything is eaten at
this meal, it is no more than a roll or
bread with butter, honey or jam.

Lunch or *yevma* is the main meal,
and it is eaten at home between noon
and 2 or 3 p.m. Appetizers, meat or fish
and salad, yogurt with honey and fruit
are typical midday meals. Wine, beer and water are common drinks for
lunch. Coffee is customarily served afterward. In villages, the midday
meal is often followed by an afternoon rest during which time schools
and businesses close.

Dinner is *deipnon* ("DEH-eep-non") in Greek. It is usually eaten in the
late evening, perhaps as late as 10 p.m. But most Greeks have appetizers
or *mezedakia* ("mez-eth-AHK-ee-ah") in the early evening. Many little
dishes of olives, various cheeses, freshly baked breads and little bits of
grilled lamb or broiled fish are routinely served. Family dinners might
consist of the same food as lunch, but sweets will be served after the fruit
course.

Greeks often go out for dinner to a local *tavérna.* Rather than looking
at a menu to make their selections, customers go right into the kitchen to
see what is cooking and what looks good!

Above: **Many restaurants
in Greece cater to
tourists and local
residents alike. In less
urban areas, eating out
is not so common as in
the towns.**

Opposite: **Poseidon's
harvest from the Medi-
terranean Sea. Greece is
famous for its fresh sea-
food.**

TABLE MANNERS AND SOCIAL GRACES

Because hospitality is considered a basic aspect of Greek culture and a natural extension of the Hellenic personality, there are no hard rules for manners. As in any culture, however, there are certain matters of etiquette that are observed.

- Dinner guests are expected to arrive 30 minutes late.
- At a meal, the male guest of honor is seated to the right of the hostess, while female guests are seated to the right of the host.
- The oldest guest is served first.
- Bread is placed on the table; there are no bread and butter plates.
- Hands do not rest on the lap and wrists must be kept on the table. In informal company, the elbows can rest on the table.
- Guests must eat a great deal to avoid offending the host.
- It is not unusual for close friends or relatives to eat from one another's plate.
- One of the most important things that a guest can do is compliment the host and hostess on the appearance of their home. The wife spends many hours preparing for guests and feels very disappointed if no mention is made of it.

GREEK COFFEE

The Greeks drink a dark, rich, finely ground coffee called *kafedaki* ("kahf-ed-AHK-ee"). It is traditionally brewed in a long-handled pot known as a *briki*. *Briki* pots come in two, four or six *demitasse* cup sizes. Greek coffee is not made in larger quantities because the foam at the top, which is supposed to bring good luck, will not be of the correct consistency. The coffee is served plain, moderately sweet or very sweet, and is accompanied by a glass of cold water.

Kafedaki is sipped carefully to avoid disturbing the grounds that settle to the bottom of the cup. A favorite pastime is to leave a little liquid in the cup, invert it on the saucer and let it dry. Fortune-tellers, who specialize in reading the future from the pattern of the dried grounds, are ever-present to provide a window to the future.

YIASSAS

The national drink of Greece is *ouzo*, which is a clear spirit that is distilled from the residue of the grapes after the wine is made. It looks as innocent as water, but has a strong licorice flavor, and can have a 50% alcohol content. It is usually drunk straight, although some people prefer to add an ice cube, which instantly turns the liquid milky white.

Retsina, a classic wine of Greece, has a very tangy resin taste. It is believed by some that the wine was originally stored in casks made of pine, which leaked resin. Others say that the resin was a preservative and Greeks just grew accustomed to the taste over the years. Still others say that the resin helps in the digestion of oily, rich foods.

When toasting each other, don't forget to smile and say, "Yiassas."

Before the first sip of an alcoholic beverage, Greeks always clink their glasses against those of their friends and make a toast. Usually they exclaim, "*yiassas*," ("yee-AHS-as") which means, "your health."

123

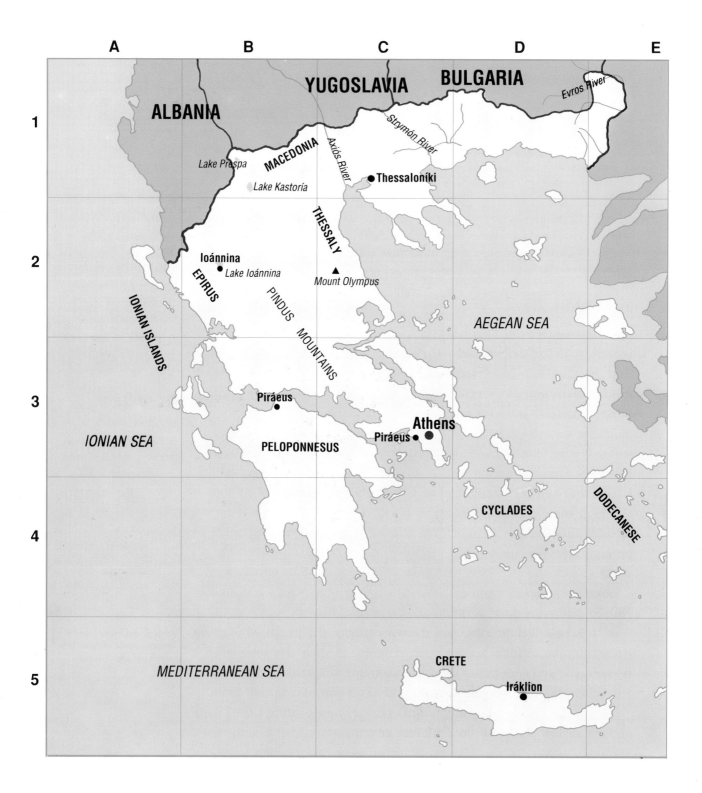

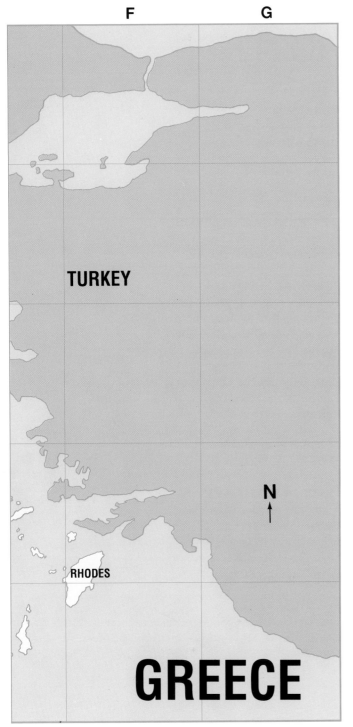

F   G

TURKEY

RHODES

N

GREECE

Aegean Sea D2	Kastoría Lake B1
Albania B1	
Athens C3	Macedonia B1
Axiós River C1	Mediterranean Sea B5
Bulgaria D1	Olympus Mount C2
Crete D5	Rhodes F4
Cyclades D4	
	Pátras B3
Dodecanese E4	Peloponnesus B3
	Pindus Mountains B2
Epirus B2	Piráeus C3
Evros River E1	Prespa lake B1
Ioánnina B2	Strymón River C1
Ioánnina Lake B2	
Ionian Islands A2 B3	Thessaloníki C1
Ionian Sea A3	Thessaly C2
Iráklion D5	Turkey F2
	Yugoslavia C1

——	International Boundary
▲	Mountain
●	Capital
●	City
〜	River
▨	Lake

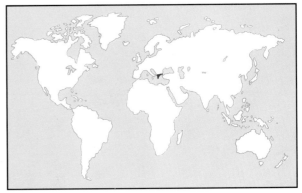

QUICK NOTES

LAND AREA
50,944 square miles

POPULATION
10 million

CAPITAL
Athens

GEOGRAPHICAL REGIONS
Aegean Islands, Central Greece, Crete, Epirus, Ionian Islands, Macedonia, Peloponnesus, Thessaly, Thrace

MOUNTAIN RANGES
Pindus Mountains

HIGHEST POINT
Mount Olympus (9,570 feet)

MAJOR TOWNS
Agrínion, Dráma, Ioánnina, Iráklion, Kalámai, Kateríni, Kaválla, Kérkira, Khaniá, Komotiní, Lárisa, Mitilíni, Rhodes, Piráeus, Patras, Sérrai, Thessaloníki, Tríkkala, Véroia, Vólos, Xánthi

NATIONAL ANTHEM
Imnos pros tin Eleftherian ("The Hymn to Liberty")

NATIONAL LANGUAGE
Greek

MAJOR RELIGION
Christianity (Greek Orthodox)

CURRENCY
100 lepta per drachma
(US$1 = 188 drachma)

MAIN EXPORTS
Olives, olive oil, textiles and tobacco

IMPORTANT ANNIVERSARIES
Independence Day (March 25)
Ochi Day (October 28)

SEASONAL FESTIVALS
Folklore Festival at Eléfsis (May)
Flower Festival at Gastouni (May)
Rhodes Festival (May–October)
Athens Festival (June–September)
Music Festival at Ithaca (July)
Crete International Festival (July–August)
Sun and Stone Festival at Kavála (July–August)
Epídaurus Festival (July–September)
Daphne Wine Festival (July–September)
Olympus Festival at Kateríni (August)
Thessaloníki Dimitria Festival (October)

LEADERS IN THE ARTS
Nikos Kazantzakis (writer)
George Seferis (poet)
Odysseus Elytis (poet)
Mikos Theodorakis (composer)
Spyros Vikatos (artist)

POLITICAL LEADERS
Constantine Caramanlis—current president
Constantine Mitsotakis—current prime minister

GLOSSARY

anchorite	One who lives in seclusion for religious reasons.
autonomous	Having the right or power of self-government.
cenobitic	Members of a religious group who live together in a monastery.
foustanella	Traditional Greek costume worn by the Greek Palace Guards.
icon	A conventional religious image painted on a small wooden panel.
insular	Surrounded by water.
kafeneíon	A Greek coffeehouse.
kéfi	A feeling of happiness and well-being.
Primate	A bishop who heads a diocese.
spelt	Wheat with light-red kernels.
synod	An ecclesiastical counsel that governs or advises.
tavérna	A Greek restaurant.
triangulation	A trigonometric operation for finding a position or location.

BIBLIOGRAPHY

Antiniou, Jim: *Greece, The Land and its People*, Silver Burdett, Morristown, N.J., 1974.
Campbell, John and Sherrard, Phillip: *Modern Greece*, Praeger, New York, 1968.
Dicks, T.R.B.: *The Greeks, How They Live and Work*, Praeger, New York, 1971.
Gage, Nicholas: *Hellas, A portrait of Greece*, Villard Books, New York, 1987.
Lyle, Garry: *Let's visit Greece*, Burke Publishing Co., Bridgeport, Conn., 1983.
U.S. Department of State, Washington D.C.: *Background Notes: Republic of Greece*.

INDEX

Acropolis 13, 94
Aeschylus 20, 89
Albanians 51
Alexander, King 27
Alexander the Great 14, 22, 90,
  96
Archaic Period 93
Aristophanes 20, 89, 117

Balkan War 27
body language 85
Byzantine Empire 24, 90, 98

Caramanlis, Constantine 29
Carnival 114
cheese 117, 118
Christmas 110
church 26, 71, 73, 78, 110
Classical Period 19, 94
coffee 63, 117, 121, 123
Constantine, King 27
Constantine II, King 33
Constantinople 24, 25, 71, 90
Cyprus 29, 33, 35

Dark Ages 18
dimotiki 83, 84, 97
dowry 66
drama 107

Easter 114
English language 84
Epiphany 112
Euripides 20, 89, 117
European Community 32, 37,
  42, 45

firewalking 79
folk costumes 55
folk dances 102, 103
funerals 69

Geometric Period 92
George I, King 27
George II, King 28

Golden Age 87, 89
gypsies 53

Herodotus 89
Hesiod 74, 88, 117
Homer 74, 88, 117
honor 62

icon 73, 78
Iliad 17, 18, 74, 88, 102

Jews 52

katharévousa 83, 84, 97
Kazantzakis, Nikos 97

marriage 60, 66
Minoans 17
military 28, 32, 35
Mitsotakis, Constantine 29
monarchy 27, 28, 31
monks 76, 77
Mount Olympus 8, 74
music 98, 101
Mycenaeans 18

Name Day 113

Odyssey 17, 74, 88
olives 10, 40
Olympics 105
Otho, Prince 27, 31, 32
Ottoman Empire 25, 26, 73, 97

Papadópoulos, George 28
Papandreou, Andreas 29
Papandreou, Geogios 33
PASOK 29, 34
Peloponnesian War 20
Pericles 21
Persians 19
Piráeus 12, 15
Plato 20, 89
Plutarch 90
pottery 99

priests 76
Primate of Greece 76

rivers 8
Roman Empire 23, 82

sculpture 92, 93, 94
shipping 72
Slavs 51, 81
smog 12
soccer 104
Socrates 20, 89
Sophocles 20, 89
Sparta 20, 92

Theogony 74, 88
Thessaloníki 14, 52
Treaty of Adrianople 27
Treaty of London 27
Turks 43, 49, 81

United States of America, The
  28, 48

Vlachs 50, 81

worry beads 64